INSIDE COLOUR

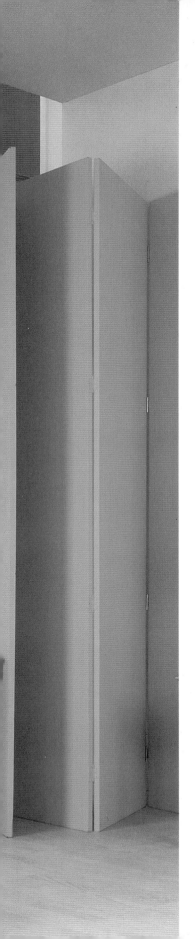

INSIDE COLOUR

The Secrets of Interior Style

Lesley Taylor

CASSELL & CO.
LONDON

To my wonderful family who have given me so much encouragement while I have been writing this book and to Sheila, Sian and Jane for all their practical help and support.

My heartfelt thanks to Rosie for her total dedication to this project and to Emma, Sarah and everybody else involved.

First published in the United Kingdom in 2000 by Cassell & Co.

Distributed in the United States of America by
Sterling Publishing Co., Inc.
387 Park Avenue South
New York NY 10016-8810

A CIP catalogue record for this book is available from the British Library

ISBN 0-304-35424-4

Designed by Ruth Prentice
Edited by Emma Scattergood
Proofread by Sarah Chatwin

Printed and bound in Italy by New Interlitho

Cassell & Co.
Wellington House
125 Strand
London WC2R 0BB

CONTENTS

INTRODUCTION

If you yearn for more confidence when it comes to choosing colours for your home, or wish you could mix and match patterns more successfully, read on. This book has been devised to help you understand the unique characteristics of colour and pattern, and gain the ability and flair to use them successfully in your own home.

Part One introduces the worlds of colour and pattern. First, we look in detail at colour and how it works. We explore the colour wheel and primary, secondary and tertiary colours are explained. We gain an understanding of tone and how it can be used. Then each colour is looked at in depth, discussing its individual merits and character.

Secondly, pattern is examined in Part One. It is broken down into categories to make it easier to understand and, of course, to apply. We explore the various qualities associated with each pattern type, describe what other patterns work well with it, and how each one has evolved through history. This will provide you with the skill to mix and match patterns for a professional look, as well as the ability to recreate the various regional and historical styles that are so popular today such as Scandinavian or oriental.

This part concludes by discussing the theory behind the decorative schemes used by professional interior designers – the trade secrets! We explain how to create each type of scheme successfully in your own home, and which ones will suit the rooms you are intending to decorate.

Part Two looks at colour and pattern within its natural surroundings in the home. This section will give you an excellent insight into the best types of pattern and colour for any individual room, from the living room to the bathroom – including a chapter dedicated to home offices and another to children's bedrooms. Once you have absorbed all this information, you will feel ready to create stylish and creative decorative schemes of your own.

If, however, you feel drawn to a certain style from another time or place, then Part Three will prove both useful and inspirational. This section takes you step by step through various historical and regional styles, identifying the particular patterns and colours that combine to create these charismatic interiors so that you can reproduce sympathetic representations of your own.

The book is designed to be dipped into as well as read from cover to cover. Use it to develop your knowledge in a certain area when it is appropriate, then pick it up again to help you finalize a scheme or work on another room. By cross-referencing the individual sections, you have a broad range of starting points. If, for example, you wish to create an authentic Victorian look, Part Three will give you an insight into that style. Your knowledge can then be extended by looking at how different patterns were used and developed in that period in Part One, while Part Two will help apply your new skills on a room-by-room basis.

There are also plenty of practical tips. We show you how to use colour and pattern to solve everyday problems, such as decorating a small, dark room, or making a narrow room feel wider. If you have to base your new scheme around an existing piece, such as a sofa or carpet, we show you how to make the most of it – refer to the section on the relevant colour or pattern of the object. For instance, if you were starting with a striped sofa, refer to Using Geometric Pattern.

I hope this book will become an invaluable and inspirational decorating tool for you. I certainly enjoyed writing it and I hope you will find it as enjoyable to read.

Happy decorating!

1

INTRODUCING COLOUR AND PATTERN

THE BASIC PRINCIPLES
of using colour

Colour is powerful and inspirational. It brings vibrancy to our world, gives everything it graces a unique character and is capable of changing the mood of those who see it.

Colour is all around us. You have been reacting to and stimulated by the different colours around you from the day you were born. If we look outside the room we are decorating for inspiration, we are certainly spoilt for choice. Nature is a good place to start. Every day it combines the yellow sun, a myriad of different greens in grasses, trees and plants, and a sky which could be anything from the most ominous black and grey to the softest palest blue. And that is just the beginning. Think of all your favourite flowers or the depths of the blue-green ocean with thousands of brightly coloured fish. Think of other animals too – a pig, a giraffe, the peacock – and the different landscapes around the world from the sparkling white of Antarctica to the reddest desert of Arizona. Consider the different seasons too, from the fresh soft palette of spring, through bright and bold summer, to the rich, warm golden tones of autumn and the neutral browns and greys of winter. Colour is everywhere in nature, but it is everywhere else too, from science and art to fashion and the supermarket. Walk down your street and vibrant colour will jump out at you: a front door, a post box, or a truck driving past.

To harness the full power of colour, however, you do need to understand the principles of colour theory. Learning the science of colour may sound rather tedious and even a little daunting, but in fact it can be a very enjoyable and enlightening process. It is rewarding to discover the reasoning behind the successful blending of colours, and reassuring to discover that many of the things you may have been doing instinctively with colour actually correspond with the theory. If at any point you find that you are unfamiliar with the terminology being used, please turn to the Glossary on page 39.

Left: COLOUR IS THE SINGLE MOST POWERFUL TOOL AVAILABLE TO THE HOME DECORATOR. IT CAN ALTER THE APPEARANCE OF THE PROPORTIONS OF A ROOM AND CAN ALSO ANCHOR A SCHEME IN A GIVEN PERIOD OR REGIONAL STYLE. UNDERSTAND COLOUR THEORY AND YOU WILL BE ABLE TO CREATE COLOUR SCHEMES THAT ARE PLEASING TO THE EYE, BUT THAT ALSO MAKE THE MOST OF THE ROOM IN WHICH THEY ARE APPLIED.

How Colour Works

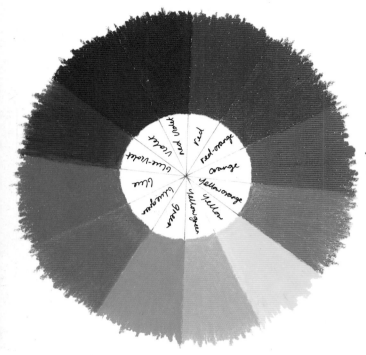

Above: Warm colours can be both welcoming and cosy, and can be used to create comfortable and casual colour schemes. Colours chosen from this side of the wheel can be either bright and stimulating or soft and easy on the eye, depending on the tone of the colour chosen.

The modern understanding of colour began in 1666, when Sir Isaac Newton proved that colour is a property of light. He projected a small beam of sunlight through a prism and displayed the emerging bands of colour onto a white screen. The colours that appeared were red, orange, yellow, green, blue and violet.

In 1770, scientist Moses Harris created the first colour wheel to define red, yellow and blue as the three primary colours – in other words, a colour that cannot be created by the mixing of other colours. The theory of colour was further extended in the early twentieth century when Johannes Itten additionally classified colour into secondary and tertiary classifications.

To best explain this modern understanding, I have chosen to use the 12-hue colour wheel system. All colours are derived from the three primary colours: red, yellow and blue. By mixing each primary colour with one other, you produce the three secondary colours. Red and yellow make orange, blue and red make violet, and yellow and blue make green.

To create a 12-hue colour wheel, take the primary and secondary colours as six of the twelve hues. The primary colours should be equally spaced around the

wheel, with the secondary colours positioned between their parent colours. This leaves six blank spaces on the wheel. These are the natural home to our six intermediate or tertiary colours. These are produced by mixing together one primary and its neighbouring secondary colour. This will produce yellow-orange, red-orange, red-violet, blue-violet, blue-green and yellow-green. When all 12 colours are correctly positioned on the wheel they create what is known as a natural spectrum.

The wheel can be further extended to a 24-hue wheel. For example, between yellow and orange you could have a natural spectrum order of: yellow (Y) the primary; yellow-orange-yellow, which is made up of two parts yellow to one part orange (YOY); yellow-orange (YO), the intermediate colour; orange-yellow-orange, which is two parts orange, one part yellow (OYO); followed by orange (O), a secondary colour.

Warm and cool

Another way of looking at and usefully dividing up the wheel is to view it in terms of warm and cool colour spectrums. Generally speaking, red, yellow and orange are considered warm colours, while blue and green are considered cool colours. Violet, however, can appear warm or cool depending on the proportions of its parent colours. A hue of violet with a large proportion of blue would appear cool, while a violet with a primarily red base would appear warm. Its appearance will also alter depending on the colours you decide to use with it. Team violet with cool blues and it will appear warmer than if you combined it with warm reds for example.

Warm colours 'advance', which means that they make any wall they are painted on appear nearer to you than it actually is. Therefore, you should use them to create cosy colour schemes, where maintaining a sense of spaciousness is not important.

Cool colours, on the other hand, 'recede', making a room painted in them look larger and also slightly more formal. You can use this knowledge to balance badly

proportioned rooms by painting or covering an awkwardly placed wall in a different colour to the adjacent walls to make it appear better positioned, be that closer to you or further away from you. For example, an extremely long and narrow room, with large windows on one of the end walls, can become more balanced with the help of colour. Warm colours used for curtaining or as blocks of colour on the two short walls, can be combined with cooler colours on the remaining two longer walls. The warm colours on the short walls opposite each other will have the effect of drawing together those two walls, while having cool colours painted on the longer facing walls will make them appear further away from each other. The overall effect is for the long walls to appear shorter and the narrow space to feel wider.

The Effect of Colour and Tone on a Space

BOTH DIFFERENT COLOURS AND DIFFERENT TONES OF COLOURS CAN BE USED TO AESTHETICALLY ALTER THE APPEARANCE OF A ROOM OR SPACE IN THE HOME. HERE ARE SOME GUIDELINES:

LIGHT COLOURS ARE REFLECTIVE AND MAKE A ROOM APPEAR LARGER.

TO MAKE A ROOM APPEAR SMALLER AND COSIER, USE WARM COLOURS.

A WALL PAINTED IN A DARK OR WARM COLOUR WILL ADVANCE, APPEARING NEARER.

COOL COLOURS RECEDE. USE THEM TO MAKE A SPACE APPEAR AS LARGE AS POSSIBLE.

A FLOOR DECORATED IN A DARK COLOUR WILL MAKE THE AREA APPEAR SMALLER.

PAINT THE CEILING DARKER IN TONE THAN THE WALLS AND IT WILL APPEAR LOWER.

PAINT THE CELING LIGHTER IN TONE THAN THE WALLS AND IT WILL APPEAR HIGHER.

IN A LARGE ROOM, LOWER THE CEILING BY PAINTING IT AND THE FRIEZE IN A DEEP TONE.

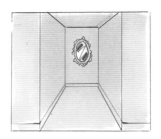

TO MAKE A HALLWAY APPEAR AS LARGE AS POSSIBLE, DECORATE IN LIGHT TONES.

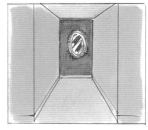

TO SHORTEN A CORRIDOR, PAINT THE END WALL IN A WARM OR DARKER TONE.

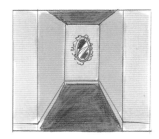

TO WIDEN A CORRIDOR, PAINT THE CEILING AND FLOOR DARKER THAN THE WALLS.

Above: TONAL VARIATION CAN BE AS IMPORTANT AS YOUR COLOUR CHOICES WITHIN A SCHEME. NEUTRAL AND MONOCHROMATIC COLOUR COMBINATIONS ARE ONLY SUCCESSFUL WHEN AMPLE CONSIDERATION IS GIVEN TO TONAL VARIATION WITHIN THE SCHEME.

Tints, shades and tones

You can add to any colour differing amounts of black and/or white to create various tints, shades and tones. Colours with just white added to the hue are known as tints. Pink, for example, is a tint of red, although it is so widely used that it has become regarded by many as a separate colour. Colours with only black added in differing quantities are known as shades.

Colours with various proportions of black and white added are known as tones. Tones of a colour are always more subdued than the original colour, which is where the saying 'toned down' originates.

Complicated as it may sound, you can now appreciate that you can have a shade of red (where black is added), but not a shade of pink. This is because pink already has white added, and so you can only have tones (where black and white are added) of pink.

Successful colour-scheming is as reliant on good use of tone as it is on colour. Tone, like colour, can also be used to alter the apparent proportions of a room. This is because, in general, the deeper the tone of a colour the less light can be reflected from it which causes the colour to appear closer than it really is. Alternatively, the lighter the tone of colour the more reflective and so the colour appears further away than it really is.

The Colour *Red*

Red is one of the three primary colours. On its positive side, we have nature's plump ripening fruit and an association with courtship and love. There is a more dangerous side, however. It is the colour of fire – assertive and passionate, hot and sometimes hard to handle.

Right: RED AND GREEN IS A VERY TRADITIONAL COMBINATION WITH A VICTORIAN AIR, AND THEY WORK EXTREMELY WELL TOGETHER IN THIS MASCULINE ENVIRONMENT.

For many years the bright red pigments used to add colour to a product or surface were very costly to produce, making red fabrics rare and expensive. A room hung with red silk drapery was seen as the height of luxury and became synonymous with stately houses and royal palaces. During the Eighties we saw a revival of primary red. It was teamed with black and white to create striking combinations. It was also used with grey, another popular colour of the time, to create slightly softer, yet very masculine colour schemes.

Now, despite its widespread availability, primary red is less popular – no doubt because people are nervous of its strength and impact. This is a shame, as red has a very warm and welcoming quality and can be used to add a dash of interest to an otherwise gentle scheme. If the prospect of using lengths of plain red fabric is rather daunting, think instead of using it in a small way – perhaps on a cushion or two, some fringing on your curtains, or by using a fabric with a thread of red running through it. Red is one of the strongest accent colours available to the home decorator, and in its purest form, it can offer contrast in a striking way. A small amount of red or pink can add a great deal of character to the quietest of schemes or bring a contemporary twist to a traditional colour scheme, without requiring too much confidence to use.

Red colour schemes

When looking for colour combinations, I very often turn to nature for my inspiration. Red plays a prominent part in the colours of the natural world, most often accompanied by a bright leaf green. Think of a ripe apple on a tree, or wild poppies in a green field. This strong colour combination works just as well in the home, particularly in a traditional setting.

This sitting room shows how red and green can create a Victorian-style interior, with a masculine air. The colour scheme has to be carefully chosen for a room like this as the colours need to reflect the traditional atmosphere of the room. Consideration should be given to tonal values to ensure that the mahogany wall panels and bookshelves do not overpower the finished room. These historical shades of red and green offer the perfect solution to both problems while the striped sofa in the foreground serves to unite the two-coloured scheme, marrying both colours in a blended look.

Note also how pattern has been used in this room. The traditional floral single-coloured wallpaper makes a good solid background for the broad two-coloured stripe of the sofa. Pictorial tapestry cushions introduce additional colour and interest to the scheme, while the small green paisley cushions offer a differing scale of

Above: RED HAS BEEN USED HERE TO SUPPLY THIS VERY ELEGANT WHITE DINING ROOM WITH A WONDERFUL SPLASH OF ACCENT COLOUR. WITHOUT THE RED, THE OVERALL EFFECT WOULD HAVE BEEN FAR LESS STRIKING AND DRAMATIC.

Above right: RED IS A POPULAR COMPONENT OF PLAIDS AND PAISLEY FABRICS, WHICH LOOK EQUALLY AT HOME IN A GRAND OR INFORMAL SETTING. BOTH THESE FABRICS ARE TRADITIONAL, WITH STRONG LINKS WITH THE VICTORIAN ERA, BUT WHEN LAYERED IN THIS WAY CREATE A VERY WELCOMING ENVIRONMENT.

pattern to maintain a balance. The secret of successful pattern-mixing is to use a variation in the scale and density of pattern (see The Basic Principles of Using Pattern, page 40). For example, the rug in the living room on the previous page introduces pattern on a much larger scale, which completes the overall scheme.

If you want to create a look that is more fresh, then combining red and white is a simple solution. Red and white have been teamed together repeatedly through-out history, in porcelain, wallpaper and fabric designs. However, it is the pattern of the red and white fabrics and wallpapers you use, as much as the colours, that

will define the finished look. Red and white gingham, for example, creates an unfussy, homely atmosphere. However, red and white toile de Jouy will produce a very different, much more elegant air.

Red and gold always make a regal and opulent combination, evocative of eastern richness, as seen in many oriental pieces of porcelain or artefacts. The Victorians loved deep red and gold, perhaps because of the associations with wealth, which the middle classes of that era took great pleasure in displaying. Whatever the reason for its popularity, it became a favoured colour combination for the rooms in which they entertained. All

shades, tones and tints of red look wonderful by candlelight, especially when enhanced by gold. This makes it the perfect colour for rooms used mainly in the evening, such as dining rooms, romantic bedrooms and formal living rooms.

This comfortable study (right) has been created by combining shades of red with traditional blue and green. It has a strong historical feel, with plaid and paisley designs linking it with the Victorian period. Terracotta shades of red ensure that the room is warm and inviting, while a brighter red is used in some objects to inject life into the overall scheme.

The Colour *Violet*

Violet, often known as purple, is a secondary colour on the colour wheel, produced by mixing red and blue. In its deepest shades it is an opulent colour associated with the Church and royalty, while its lighter tints, such as soft lilac, lavender and foxglove, create a tranquil air of spirituality and sensuality – ideal for rooms dedicated to relaxation and contemplation.

Purple has repeatedly been seen as a popular colour for home decorating. In my lifetime alone I have seen it become the height of fashion in three different decades. There is currently a strong connection being drawn between fashion and interior design, due to the interest now being shown by fashion designers in the interiors market. However, if you look back over the last 30 years, the link between the colours used on the catwalk and those that dress our homes was already more than evident.

In the Sixties, flower power spilled from fashion into interiors, bringing with it many of its favoured colourways – one being purple. The mid-Seventies saw the introduction of a stronger shade of purple used in blocks on individual walls which were normally surrounded by simple white paintwork. The late Nineties saw yet another revival of this colour. This time it was introduced into furnishing fabrics and wallcoverings in

lighter harmonious combinations, such as aquamarine and purple or soft green and lavender, for looks which are much less demanding.

Violet colour schemes

Violet is sited on the colour wheel at the point where cool and warm meet, and because its parent colours (blue and red) have an almost equal strength of colour it can be either warm or cool, making it a versatile colour for the interior decorator. If the shade of violet you choose is predominantly blue it will appear cool, whereas if it has a mainly red base it will appear warm. Certain shades and tones of violet can be very intense, and should therefore be treated with respect and used cautiously. Pale shades like lavender, however, are fresh and uplifting – the perfect colour to add vitality to a country scheme. Lavender works beautifully with white, giving a room a crisp freshness; or it can add a contemporary twist to a room, when teamed with yellow, green or sharp lime.

When looking for other colours to combine with purple, you need not go much further than pink. Pink being a red tint (that is red with white added), it sits next to violet on the colour wheel, making pink and violet a harmonious colour partnership (see Harmonious Colour Schemes, page 68). Tones of purple will also sit very comfortably with various tones of green – a good colour combination for a light and feminine, but not too fussy, bedroom.

Right: THE COLOURS YOU CHOOSE MAY MAKE A DESIGN STATEMENT IN THEMSELVES, BUT ADD SOME TEXTURAL INTEREST TOO AND THE SCHEME TAKES ON ANOTHER DIMENSION. HERE THE COMBINATION OF TEXTURAL FABRICS, SUCH AS LINEN, AND THE UP-TO-THE-MINUTE COLOURS HAVE PRODUCED A STYLISH LIVING ROOM SCHEME.

A successful combination with a more contemporary feel is violet and aquamarine. Various shades and tints of blue are naturally harmonious partners for purple, again because they sit next to each other on the colour wheel. The very stylish dining room shown here demonstrates how combining tints of aquamarine and purple can produce a relaxing and calm environment. In a contemporary setting like this one, silver accessories work perfectly – their chic, cooling qualities sit well with the cool-coloured tints of the walls and the furniture. Introducing gold accessories, which are warm-coloured, into the same environment would break the harmony of the scheme. However, the whole room does benefit from the addition of an acidic green accent, which adds some vitality to the scheme.

Green is a colour universally accepted as being an excellent partner for most, if not all, other colours on the colour wheel, and purple is no exception. The combination of these colours can create a fresh country-style atmosphere. You can think beyond purple in its purest forms and include its red or blue tones as well. The toile de Jouy fabric is a perfect example of a fabric which often appears in red purple. It is extremely traditional and would work well in a historical setting, given the backdrop of a more historical palette. Combined with a soft green though, it would create a more informal country feel. This goes to prove, once again, that it is the complete scheme – the combination of colour, pattern and style – that provide a room with its atmosphere or theme; one pattern or colour reference is not enough to finish the look.

Left: Pastel shades are colours to which a generous amount of white has been added to create a pale tint of the original. The full spectrum of pastel colours will always work well together in any combination and is the only complete family of colours that can be relied on for doing this. Here pastel aquamarine and soft purple combine harmoniously for a contemporary dining room.

The Colour *Blue*

Blue is a primary colour. Bold, bright and dynamic or cool, peaceful and refreshing, it is a colour that is easy to live with and often a favourite. In nature, it is the colour of cornflowers, rockpools and the deepest ocean. Think also of the Mediterranean where blue is at its brightest and most vibrant in the splashes of paintwork and the sun-filled sky.

In interiors, blue is often used as a formal colour, probably because it adds a cool quality to a room. This will give a space a feeling of calm, but it will not be as welcoming as one decorated in the warm colours from the colour wheel. It is classed as a receding colour, giving the illusion of space, so it is also the perfect colour for making a room appear airy and expansive.

Blue colour schemes

Blue is easy to use in the home, not least because it partners successfully with so many other colours. White is a traditional partner for blue, a combination seen repeatedly in blue and white porcelain (such as the oriental designs and Wedgwood) and fabrics. The combination is fresh and vital, and with the different uses of pattern can be used to create a contemporary look, a sharp formality, or a more rustic, home-spun air. Look at blue-and-white stripes, toile de Jouy, ginghams and florals, to see the different effects that can be achieved.

For a more harmonious partnership, try blue and green, a coupling echoed frequently in nature by fresh blue flowers with their green leaves and stems. These colours offer a very balancing atmosphere to a room, and when used with paler tones of colour they create an extremely tranquil yet focused environment, ideal for a bedroom or study.

To make a stronger contrast, look to add red as an accent in a mainly blue colour scheme. Pure reds contrast well with deeper blues for a strong look, and tints of red, in the form of pink, are a wonderful partner for paler blues in more subtle surroundings.

Yellow and blue is always a popular combination. These contrasting colours from the opposite sides of the colour wheel offer a vibrant yet balanced mix. When seen in their purest, strongest form they add vitality to a room – imagine the summer sun in a Mediterranean blue sky – or for a softer look think in terms of pastel lemons and a paler sky blue to add warmth and softness. Yellow and blue work best together when the colours are tonally equal.

Above: THIS COLOUR SCHEME IS QUITE UNUSUAL IN THAT IT RELIES PURELY ON ONE TONE OF BLUE FOR ITS FURNISHINGS. BE CAUTIOUS ABOUT ADOPTING THIS APPROACH YOURSELF. A SCHEME IS MORE INTERESTING AND EASIER ON THE EYE IF IT INCLUDES A RANGE OF TONAL VALUES. HERE, HOWEVER, A SUBTLE VARIATION WILL BE ACHIEVED WITH THE LIGHT CAST FROM THE BEDSIDE LAMPS.

The dining room on the left is vibrant and stylish. Here we can see mid-blue used to great effect with a slightly acidic yellow.

As already mentioned, blue is a receding colour and tends to push back the walls it covers, making the area seem larger than it is. But as you look at this dining room you may understandably question this information. You can probably think of other colours that would have helped to make this room appear larger than it does at present – and they would all undoubtedly be of a lighter tone than the blue featured here. This goes to prove the impact tonal value has on a space, and the importance of considering tone and colour equally.

As I said earlier in this section (page 14), in general, the deeper the tone of colour you choose the less light can be reflected from it and the colour will appear closer; or conversely, the lighter the tone of colour, the more reflective it becomes and the colour will appear further away. Imagine the walls of this room decorated in a terracotta or green of the same tone as the blue currently used. The space would automatically be drawn in, and appear smaller. Out of the two, terracotta would have the greatest effect on the space. This is because green is made up of blue and yellow, and so inherits some of its blue parent's cooler receding qualities. Terracotta, however, does not contain blue and, therefore, does not have any of its receding properties. So remember, when comparing the power of colour you must choose colours of an equal tonal value.

Do not be put off using deeper tones of blue purely because you are worried about the apparent effect it will have on the size of the room. If you are decorating a dining area that is used for entertaining in the evening, mid- to dark blue tones are the perfect option. Illuminated by candlelight or with carefully placed accent lighting, these tones of blue will actually give the room an extremely expansive atmosphere – almost as if you were surrounded by a summer's night sky.

Because the most aesthetically pleasing combinations of yellow and blue are tonally equal, you must be careful when planning your decor to ensure that the finished room has adequate tonal interest. A room that is decorated completely in colours of an equal tonal value can be flat, uninteresting, and have very little definition. This room (left) has none of these problems. While the blue and yellow used is of an almost equal tonal value, the upholstery fabric combining these two colours also includes a stripe of a darker, almost black, blue. This same blue is used to bring definition to the window via a simple fringe-edged drape, while the white star-patterned voile at the window, the white painted floor and the crisp lightshades all supply a tonal contrast to the mid-blue walls. The room manages to retain its fresh atmosphere because the majority of colour (and non-colour, such as white) is lighter than the blue. Even the console table and wooden-legged chairs are a pale, yellow-cream timber. This leaves the darker tonal contrast to the thin table frame, the simple window drape and the decorative terracotta pots.

As with many colour schemes, this room has benefited from the introduction of a third colour. The red featured in the painting may not appear an important part of the decor, but in fact it has a very powerful effect on the appearance of the finished room, adding life and vitality into a well planned decorative scheme.

Left: THIS BLUE AND YELLOW SCHEME IS PERFECTLY BALANCED IN COLOUR AND TONE. WHEN PLANNING A COLOUR SCHEME TONE ADDS DEPTH AND DEFINITION, WHILE COLOUR ADDS ATMOSPHERE AND LIFE TO THE ROOM.

Above: THIS CHILD'S BEDROOM IS THE IDEAL HAVEN FOR YOUR LITTLE ONES TO DRIFT OFF TO SLEEP IN, AS COOL COLOURS LIKE THIS BLUE HAVE A CALMING QUALITY. THE USE OF TRADITIONAL BLUE AND WHITE FABRICS GIVES THIS ROOM A NOSTALGIC AIR.

The Colour *Green*

Green is a secondary colour, produced by mixing blue and yellow. Easy on the eye and relaxing, it is very versatile, as many tones and shades of green can be combined within one colour scheme. In nature, there is endless inspiration for green colour schemes, as numerous varieties can be seen at every turn. Think of apple, grass, lime, sage and avocado green and consider how naturally they can be paired with red, earthy browns, bright yellows and the colours of spring flowers.

Green, like violet, is sited on the colour wheel between a cool and a warm parent – blue and yellow. However, because blue dominates the mix, green is considered a cool colour – with the exception of very yellow lime, which has a sharp brightness.

Because green is derived from the mixing of two such total opposites, it is also a very balanced colour and will create a very steadying and contemplative room, ideal for calming nerves. It is this quality that has led it to be used for decorating 'green rooms', where actors go to prepare and relax in the theatre, and that also makes it the ideal choice for studies and home offices, where concentration is important.

Green colour schemes

Greens with a very yellow base, such as lime, have an uplifting quality. Rather like the yellow-green shoots of new young leaves, they create an optimistic and fresh atmosphere. The contemporary living room seen here has an acidic green for its basic colour scheme combined with simply painted floorboards for an airy and expansive look. The walls have been papered using a dragged effect wallpaper that also features contemporary repeat motifs and a stylized stripe design, all in a lighthearted freehand style to emphasize the young and casual feel of the room.

Green is one colour that combines well with any tone, shade or tint of the same colour, so although the pendant light featured in the foreground of this picture is of a different shade of green, it sits very well in the overall scheme.

If you want a green that is more restful than uplifting, look towards the blue-based side of the spectrum. Greens with a blue base, such as aquamarine, take on some of the restful qualities of their blue parent colour. Calming and reflective, aquamarine is ideal to use in a room dedicated to total relaxation, such as the bedroom or the bathroom. Blue-based greens are particularly popular at the moment and can be seen frequently in contemporary-style interiors. However, they have been used throughout history and have connections with regional-style interiors such as the Swedish Gustavian look (see Scandinavian Style in Part Three, page 184)

where soft duck-egg blue, a colour with a green under-tone, is used widely.

For successful colour combinations within a green scheme, you can look to almost all areas of the colour wheel. As in nature, green works well with most other colours, giving you a free rein in your choice.

For harmonious colour combinations, look for colours that lie adjacent to green on the colour wheel. Green, blue-green and yellow-green offer a very relax-ing scheme. If you want to make more of a dramatic statement, look for a contrasting colour, such as red. Directly opposite on the colour wheel, this is green's most striking contrast colour and offers a very power-ful scheme when used in its purest and strongest form. However, tints of green and red, in the form of pink and soft green, will combine to create a very delicate and complementary partnership – ideal when used in small floral-printed wallpaper and fabrics for a country-style room, or even in large blocks of solid colour in a contemporary setting.

Left: Acidic green is very uplifting. It is a colour normally associated with the younger generations as it is an inspiring, rather than calming, shade of green, with a modern feel.

Nature's colour schemes are not always fresh and bright. Consider ploughed fields and the shades of autumn for your inspiration, as much as the very first flowers of spring or the bright vitality of summer. Combining terracotta and earthy shades of burgundy with a soft green can give a room a warm glow associated with Provençal-style interiors. This elegant dining room (below) has a French feel, and while the colours chosen for the curtaining and soft furnishings could appear heavy, the softness of the pale green walls helps to balance the finished scheme and gives the room an expansive air. Pattern has been kept to a minimum, and the pieces that have been chosen to furnish this room combine with its colour scheme to create a very distinctive setting. Many people might have chosen to use the cream – seen here as a background colour in the curtain fabric – for the walls, but this would not have provided the same character or elegant atmosphere as the soft green.

For further inspiration with different greens, try thinking of beautifully presented food, such as a bowl of fresh fruit, pink fish sprinkled with herbs, a platter of vegetables, a dish of lemons and limes, or vanilla and mint ice cream. The combinations are endless.

Left: IF YOU ARE CHOOSING A WALL COLOUR TO SUPPORT A FAVOURED FABRIC AND THE COLOURS THAT ARE FEATURED WITHIN ITS DESIGN ARE NOT IDEAL, CONSIDER THE VARIOUS SHADES AND TONES OF GREEN, AS THIS NATURAL COLOUR CAN WORK SUCCESSFULLY WITH MANY OTHER COLOURS. WHILE THERE IS A FINE GREEN STRIPE WITHIN THE CURTAIN FABRIC FEATURED IN THIS DINING ROOM, IT IS NOT A PROMINENT FEATURE OF THE SCHEME AND THE GREEN WALLS WOULD HAVE WORKED EQUALLY WELL IF IT HAD NOT BEEN PRESENT IN THE SOFT FURNISHINGS.

Right: THIS SIMPLE, YET STYLISH BATHROOM HAS A STRONG ART DECO FEEL. CERAMIC TILES ADD COLOUR AND PATTERN TO THE WALLS IN AN ORDERED MANNER, BUT IT IS THE COMBINATION OF SOFT PERIOD GREEN AND GEOMETRIC BLACK DETAILING THAT GIVES THE ROOM ITS STRONG PERIOD STYLE.

The Colour *Yellow*

A primary colour, yellow is warm and welcoming and will bring light and life into the darkest or dullest of rooms. Who could fail to be cheered by the colour of bright sunlight and bobbing sunflowers? Or be inspired by the range, from fresh lemons to different mustards or the perfect sandy beach?

Right: A ROOM WITH VERY LITTLE, IF ANY, NATURAL LIGHT IS THE PERFECT SETTING FOR A YELLOW COLOUR SCHEME. THIS BATHROOM INCLUDES A NUMBER OF SHADES OF THIS COLOUR, EACH DISCREETLY HIGHLIGHTING CERTAIN ELEMENTS OF THE ROOM'S ARCHITECTURE. IN SUCH A SETTING, IT IS A GOOD IDEA TO CHOOSE A SOFT SHEEN FINISH FOR THE PAINT, AS THIS WILL HELP TO REFLECT THE SMALL AMOUNT OF DAYLIGHT THAT IS CAPTURED IN THE ROOM.

Yellow is now one of the most widely used colours in modern decorating, but it is far from being a new colour for the home decorator. Bright yellow was first introduced in the early nineteenth century and, teamed with black and warm red, it became widely used in a neo-classical setting. Prior to the introduction of the bright chrome yellow we know today, natural pigments from ochre and raw sienna were widely used to produce a more mellow but glowing range of colours, such as yellow ochre itself, saffron and mustard.

Yellow colour schemes

Yellow works successfully in most rooms around the home, and is perfect for anyone who wants to be bold with colour, but does not want the finished look to be overpowering. If used in a well balanced monochromatic scheme, yellow is strong enough to produce a substantial look that has impact but is not oppressive.

The bathroom can make a perfect setting for a yellow scheme – especially if it is a bathroom that is prone to being chilly in the mornings. The one shown here is fairly small, with little natural light, and so the wrong decoration could easily have made it claustrophobic or fussy. With this simple yellow scheme, however, the room appears spacious and stylish. As with all monochromatic schemes, its success lies in tonal variation. Here sunshine yellow meets with a warm gold on both the floor and upper wall areas, which subtly define the angular shape of the room, adding interest and form to the space. Even the woodwork has been given the yellow treatment, so that there is no break in the scheme to jar the eye or restrict the illusion of space. The silver vase of orange Gerberas finishes the look, making a feature of the window. The white bath also adds tonal interest. White will emphasize the properties of the colours next to it. Yellow looks sharper and crisper, while cream would be richer and fresher.

If you want to choose a contrasting colour for your yellow room, then look first to blue. Yellow and blue make a very balanced partnership as the colours lie directly opposite each other on the colour wheel. Coupling the two colours offers a number of styling solutions, all giving a different atmosphere to a room. Combining sunshine yellow and deep Mediterranean blue, for example, will create a vibrant, modern and uplifting look, while a room decorated in buttermilk yellow and soft china blue will be more calming and traditional. Remember, though, that yellow works best with blues of the same tonal value, or depth, as itself.

For a more harmonious partnership, look for colours that lie adjacent to yellow on the wheel, such as green. Green can act as the perfect accent in a room decorated mainly in tones of yellow through to gold. Lime will add a citric freshness to a contemporary vivid yellow setting, while a softer sage will add interest to a more traditional room.

If yellow and green, or any other harmonious colours, are used in almost equal quantities within a colour scheme, a third colour may be required to add depth and contrast to the room. In this case choose a colour that lies opposite the yellow or green on the colour wheel, such as pink or red. Adding some soft peach or earthy terracotta in a few scatter cushions, a lampshade or as a detail in a pattern will enliven a room and make it more interesting.

Pink can also be a very powerful and exciting partner for yellow. When combined they create a striking colour scheme. Again, I like to mix my yellow with a pink of an equal tonal strength. In a contemporary setting, bright yellow and cerise work wonderfully together. If the two colours are used in equal proportions, then adding a third colour, such as a splash of lime, will add that extra twist that is often needed to finish a colour scheme. For example, yellow and rose or coral pink together create a fresh and sunny traditional environment, but grass green or light avocado offer the perfect accent colours, which might be needed in such rooms. In fact, many archive floral chintz fabrics combine these three colours.

Fabrics often act as a source of inspiration when decorating a room. The colours in this traditional sitting room (left) have been influenced by the French-style curtain fabric. The predominantly yellow fabric also features pinks, blue and green. The designer has chosen to use blue as the main partner to the yellow, using

various shades from powder blue through to cornflower for the main items of upholstered furniture and for the window blinds. This leaves pink as the perfect accent for the room. An accent colour should be used in carefully positioned blocks around a room. If it is used too widely, it loses its power as an accent and becomes part of the main scheme. In general, warm colours, such as pink and red, act as a stronger accent than receding cool colours like blue.

Left: YELLOW IS A GOOD BACKDROP FOR ADDITIONAL COLOUR. HERE PINK AND BLUE ARE BOTH SEEN AGAINST SUNSHINE-YELLOW WALLS. A CURTAIN FABRIC FEATURING ALL THREE COLOURS MAY WELL HAVE BEEN THE INSPIRATION FOR THE SCHEME.

Above: YELLOW AND WHITE COMBINATIONS OFFER THE HOME DECORATOR A FRESH SUNNY PALETTE. HERE NATURAL GREEN HAS BEEN INTRODUCED AS AN ACCENT VIA THE PRETTY JUG OF GARDEN FLOWERS AND THE BOWL OF DESSERT PEARS.

The Colour *Orange*

Orange can be vital and strong. A colour seen in nature in its namesake, the ripened citrus fruit, but also in the form of the setting sun and hot flames. No wonder then that orange is a very warm colour, ideal for introducing a temperate glow to any room.

A secondary colour, orange has many of its parent colours' attributes – the cheerfulness of yellow, combined with the heat and vibrancy of red. In China and Japan, it is thought of as a sacred, happy and healthy colour, and Buddhist monks wear it to denote joy in humility. It is also a very welcoming colour, making any room it graces feel instantly warmer and more inviting.

The power of colour should not be underestimated. Not only is it an essential ingredient of home decorating, it is quite often used as a tool in personal therapy. Colour therapists recognize orange as a colour capable of stimulating the immune system and reducing pain. It has also been used as a healing agent for the treatment of ulcers and is considered to be very helpful when combating both depression and alcoholism. Of course, you may not be too concerned about the healing properties of your paint colour, but this does go to show just what an uplifting and positive colour orange is, and you should remember that when choosing your colours.

Orange can be introduced into the decorative scheme in a number of ways. Paint is an obvious choice, but there are now also plenty of orange wallcoverings available in a wide range of patterns, shades and tones. Fabrics will inevitably be the next consideration, and technical advances have led to the broadest ever colour spectrum available within fabric design, so the range of oranges to choose from is quite staggering! However, when you are considering ways of introducing orange to your scheme, you should also think beyond the man-made paints and fabrics, and consider the range of natural materials that will introduce the same shades in a softer and less synthetic way. Natural terracotta floorcoverings, for example, are ideal for both traditional and contemporary decorative schemes, and will add a Mediterranean, sun-bleached air to a room.

Orange colour schemes

Orange is a colour that should be used with caution within the home, as large blocks of it can make a room appear too intense and over-stimulating. If you decide to use orange on the walls of a room, for example, it may be wise to consider a colourwash to add softness without detracting from the warmth that orange generates. Or, rather than opting for orange at its most bright and bold, shades of orange like terracotta or apricot may be the solution.

All of orange's shades, tones and tints can be used to great effect with many other colours from the colour wheel. Pastel orange and a light green is a particularly good choice for a chilly hall. Another one is a more earthy terracotta combined with mellow green, as long as your hallway receives enough natural light, or is well lit by artificial sources.

If you want a more vibrant look, however, bright orange can be used with sky or cobalt blues, limes or violet to create a more contemporary feel. Lively and uplifting, this type of colour combination is ideal for rooms in which you socialize or spend time as a young busy family, although not so good for a room in which you want to relax.

Colour therapists warn that orange should not be used with black. When orange and black are combined they are thought to drain the emotions and warmth from a person, leaving them feeling empty and miserable – certainly not the effect anyone is looking for from a colour scheme in their home, so take heed!

Above: A COMBINATION OF
ORANGE STYLIZED FLORALS
AND GEOMETRIC PATTERNS
CREATE A BRIGHT, STIMULATING
LIVING ROOM.

Left: EARTHY SHADES OF
ORANGE ARE VERY
COMFORTING AND ADD
WARMTH TO A ROOM,
ESPECIALLY WHEN, AS HERE, IT
IS COMBINED WITH EQUALLY
WARM SHADES OF RED AND
YELLOW. THE ADDITION OF
THE NEUTRAL OR 'NON-
COLOUR' WHITE, BALANCES
THE SCHEME, PREVENTING IT
FROM BECOMING TOO
OVERPOWERING.

Rustic shades of orange can work very well in a trad-itional setting and are especially effective at making large austere rooms feel more comfortable and welcom-ing. Avoid pure orange colour in a traditional setting, as it will appear synthetic and out of place in a period or historical-style room. Colours such as terracotta or apricot are a subtler alternative, or use a colourwash finish to tone the original colour down. The relaxing lounge featured here (above left), for example, is trad-itional, yet the walls have been successfully decorated in what is quite a fashionable shade of orange. It is the eclectic blend of soft furnishings and the quirky dec-orative items used within the room that prevent the room from looking completely traditional. If the room had been accessorized with traditionally framed pic-tures and carefully chosen antique pieces of furniture, it would have taken on a different atmosphere. This shows just how versatile a colour orange can be, and how your choice of furniture and furnishings will equally dictate the effect of the finished scheme.

Another place in which you might consider introducing orange is a child's room. Because orange is such a lively and invigorating colour, it is ideal for the decoration of playrooms. Yet it is warming and comforting too, which make it appropriate for the bedroom – despite not being viewed as the most relaxing of colours on the colour wheel! True, it may not help to soothe your child to sleep at night, but this wonderful colour will have the effect of encouraging them to wake up bright and breezy, full of enthusiasm for the day ahead.

Below: A CHILD'S BEDROOM SHOULD BE A FUN PLACE. COLOURFUL TOYS AND THE PARAPHERNALIA ASSOCIATED WITH A GROWING CHILD CAN LOOK OUT OF PLACE IN CERTAIN COLOUR SCHEMES, BUT A BRIGHT AND UPLIFTING ORANGE WORKS EXTREMELY WELL AS A BACKGROUND FOR A ROOM FULL OF TOYS.

Glossary

You may not actually be familiar with much of the terminology used in this book and elsewhere in the field of decoration and design. To rectify this, here is a glossary which you can use for reference.

Accent colour This is a colour used as a highlight, to add extra interest to a scheme.

Advancing colours These are found on the warm side of the colour wheel and include red, orange and yellow. They are so called because of their ability to make a surface appear closer to the eye than it actually is.

Colourwash A decorative finish produced by the application of several layers of diluted colour, creating a luminous paint effect.

Colour Wheel A tool, based on the work of Sir Isaac Newton, which displays colours in their natural order (see page 12).

Combing A decorative paint effect achieved by drawing a comb through wet glaze.

Contrasting colours Otherwise known as complementary colours, these are colours that lie on opposite sides of the colour wheel, and when combined produce a lively contrast in a room.

Cool colours These are found opposite the advancing or warm colours on the colour wheel and include blue, green and violet.

Dado rail A decorative moulding dividing a wall at approximately the height of a chair back – originally to protect the wall.

Distemper A traditional paint produced by combining glue, water, whiting and size.

Distressed effects Paint effects or finishes which create an old, naturally worn look.

Dragging A decorative paint effect achieved by drawing a long-haired brush through wet glaze.

Eggshell An oil-based mid-sheen paint which is useful for woodwork, giving a more matt and traditional finish than gloss.

Emulsion A water-based paint for internal use on walls and floors.

Frieze A traditional band around a room, usually at or just below the cornice.

Glaze A transparent acrylic or oil-based liquid used in decorative paint techniques.

Gloss Oil-based shiny paint used mainly for wood and metalwork, both inside and outside the home.

Graining A decorative paint effect that emulates the grain of natural timber.

Harmonious colours These are colours that lie next to one another on the colour wheel, such as blue and purple.

Hue This is a word used to describe all types of colour. Tints, shades and tones of primary, secondary and tertiary colours can all be described as hues.

Intermediate colours Intermediate (or tertiary) colours are found between the primary and secondary colours on the colour wheel; for example yellow-orange.

Monochromatic colour schemes Decorative schemes produced by combining various tones of one colour.

Neutral colours Non-colours, such as white and black, as well as brown, beige and cream.

Primary colours These are red, yellow and blue, which cannot be produced by the mixing of any other colours on the colour wheel.

Rag rolling A decorative paint effect created by using a rag to apply paint or glaze.

Receding colours These are colours from the cool side of the colour wheel, named because they make a surface appear further from the eye than it really is.

Sample board A board for displaying samples of wallpapers, paints, fabrics and any other products that are intended for use in a room scheme.

Secondary colours Secondary colours are produced by the mixing of two primary colours; for example red and yellow make orange. They are found directly between the primaries on the colour wheel.

Shades Colours with some black added to make them deeper.

Tertiary colours Tertiary (or intermediate) colours are found between the primary and secondary colours on the colour wheel; for example yellow-orange.

Tints Colours with some white added to make them lighter.

Tones Colours with varying amounts of both black and white added.

Trompe l'oeil A decorative effect, usually a mural, used to create a three-dimensional image on a wall, door or piece of furniture.

Warm colours These are found opposite the cool colours on one side of the colour wheel, and include red, orange and yellow.

THE BASIC PRINCIPLES
of using pattern

The beauty of pattern is all around us – though we may not always be aware of it. Look beyond patterned fabrics and wallcoverings to the clouded sky, the leaves on a tree, or a cobblestone path. Pattern adds interest and texture to our lives outside the home, so why not incorporate it in interior decoration to enrich our lives inside the home. Nature's patterns may be regular or irregular, simple or complex, but they will always be inspirational.

In nature, pattern is combined effortlessly. Think of mounds of smooth, round pebbles merging on a coarse, sandy beach, or a long expanse of lawn, littered with small-petalled daisies. We are surrounded by a constantly changing backdrop of patterns, yet so many of us are still frightened to use, and especially to combine, patterns in our homes.

I think it is the knowledge that pattern can visually alter the proportions of an item or a space, coupled with a lack of experience, that causes this reticence – so it may boost your confidence to know that even the most seasoned of designers can be found agonizing over a choice of pattern combination for a client.

So how can anyone learn to use pattern successfully? First we must understand pattern and its various forms. The next section of this book has been specially designed to help you become familiar with various types of pattern, and gives you a guide to their uses in general, regional and historical interiors. We look at the effects each type of pattern can have on an item or space, and in some cases, look at the other patterns that work best with it. Armed with this information, you can then look again at the section dedicated to the mixing of patterns. Once you understand the principles, you will be able to use pattern with flair and confidence and create stunning schemes for your home.

Pattern can be used in one of two ways in a domestic setting: subtly, by adding some small detail and interest, perhaps in order to fix a room into a specific regional or historical style; or in a bold manner, so that the pattern becomes the main focus of the room and the eye is treated to a carnival of shapes and/or colours.

Left: PATTERN CAN BE USED TO ENHANCE A PREDETERMINED COLOUR SCHEME. HERE GEOMETRIC FLOORING AND AN OPEN FLORAL MOTIF COMPLEMENT THE YELLOW AND BLUE COLOURWAY.

Choosing the right scale of pattern

Linking the scale of pattern to the size of the area being decorated is very important. It is easy to understand why you should avoid using oversized designs in a small room, but how do you ensure that you are choosing the right pattern for the correct setting, or that a pattern which looks appropriate in the sample book will look right once it is on the walls?

One of the biggest problems home decorators have is imagining a pattern actually in the room. Wallpapers, for example, come in sample books that are a fraction of the size of the wall they will cover. While a pattern may appear quite large in a sample book, it will look considerably smaller when applied to the wall. If you are unsure what the finished effect might be, position the book against the wall and view it from the furthest position in the room. You will be amazed. Some patterns just disappear!

Repeat motifs can become a subtle ordered pattern when applied to a large surface. This is ideal in many cases, as a background to a collection of paintings or pictures, for example, and will often work extremely well if it is combined with larger designs on the curtaining or soft furnishings. However, if you have chosen a motif wallpaper to make more of an impact, then you might be disappointed.

Stripes will add height to a room. However, narrow stripes, when extremely close together, will become a blur, appearing a softer colour than the stripe itself when seen from a distance. On the other hand, broad stripes, particularly in two colours, will draw in the room, making it appear smaller than it actually is.

Pictorial patterns add drama to a room, but use them with caution as they will often dominate an area, being strong and powerful. If you use the pictorial pattern in small splashes and combine it with other styles of pattern, it will be less overpowering and will simply add visual interest.

Left: IF YOU WISH TO HIGHLIGHT A SPECIFIC AREA OR ITEM WITHIN A ROOM, USE PATTERN TO DRAW ATTENTION TO THIS PARTICULAR FEATURE AND SURROUND IT WITH PLAIN BLOCKS OF COLOUR. HERE A VERY DECORATIVE AND SUMPTUOUS SOFA IS SURROUNDED BY UNOBTRUSIVE COLOUR, MAKING IT UNDOUBTEDLY THE MAIN FEATURE OF THE ROOM. THE RESULT IS A ROOM THAT IS STILL LIGHT AND AIRY, DESPITE A HEAVILY PATTERNED CENTREPIECE.

Left: ALTHOUGH IT IS COLOUR THAT INITIALLY GIVES FORM TO A SCHEME, IT IS PATTERN THAT ADDS DEPTH AND INTEREST. ARTFULLY MIXED AND MATCHED, DIFFERENT PATTERNS CAN CREATE THE IMPRESSION OF A LOOK THAT HAS EVOLVED OVER TIME, RATHER THAN ON A SAMPLE BOARD. HERE RED AND YELLOW SET THE SCENE IN THIS STYLISH INTERIOR, WHILE THE ADDITION OF VARIOUS DIFFERENT PATTERNS IN THESE COLOURS ENSURES THE ROOM HAS AMPLE VISUAL INTEREST.

Below: THE ABILITY TO MIX PATTERN IS INVALUABLE AND THE LAYERING OF VARIOUS DESIGNS AND COLOURS IS THE VERY BACKBONE TO MANY INTERIOR STYLES. HERE FLORALS MIX WITH MOTIFS AND AN ELABORATE, BUT OPEN FLORAL-PATTERNED, WALLCOVERING TO ADD INTEREST AND COLOUR TO THIS SITTING ROOM. THE LINKING THEME BETWEEN ALL THESE DESIGNS IS THE SOFT RED, WHILE THE YELLOW CUSHION HELPS TO UNITE THE CURTAIN FABRIC WITH THE ARMCHAIR.

Mixing Patterns

Pattern falls into the following categories: geometric, floral, motif and pictorial. All of these can be woven into or printed on to the fabric or wallcovering. Single-coloured variations of many patterns, where the pattern is the same colour as the background it sits on, can be further classified as textural. This type of pattern loses many of the attributes and impact of its particular style, due to its lack of contrasting colour, but this is often more than compensated for by the addition of a sensuous tactile quality. All these categories of pattern can be mixed successfully with some thought and practice.

Interior designers are often admired for their natural ability to mix patterns successfully. There is no secret, however, to pattern-mixing and most people, when given direction, will find it easy to combine the correct type of designs. Successful pattern-combining relies on a recognition of the various families of patterns (which are examined one by one in the rest of this section) and their scale. When considering the scale of different patterns you wish to combine, you need to identify both the size of the actual pattern and the density of the background. For instance, you might have a large-sized pattern with a lot of space around it (an open background) or maybe a small repeat motif which is tightly packed together making a dense background.

Left: FLORALS ARE SYNONYMOUS WITH TRADITIONAL COUNTRY-STYLE PROPERTIES, BUT WILL STILL WORK EXTREMELY EFFECTIVELY WITHIN A MORE MODERN ENVIRONMENT. HERE A SMALL FLORAL PATTERN HAS BEEN COMBINED WITH A DECORATIVE STRIPE ON THE CURTAINING AND CHAIRS, SHOWING HOW WELL STRIPES AND FLORALS CAN SIT TOGETHER. THE COLOURS ARE UNITED WITH A SIMPLE LEMON BACKGROUND AND A SOFT BLUE TABLETOP, CREATING A STYLISH, UNFUSSY, YET FEMININE INTERIOR.

Left: PARTICULAR TYPES OF PATTERN WILL HELP TO DEFINE A REGIONAL STYLE WITHIN YOUR ROOM. THIS SWEDISH-INSPIRED BEDROOM FEATURES BLUE AND WHITE STRIPED FABRIC FOR UPHOLSTERY, WHICH IS TYPICAL OF THIS STYLE OF DECOR. PATTERN IS ALSO INTRODUCED TO THE WALLS ON HANDPAINTED PANELS WHICH, WHILE SUBTLE IN THEIR ORNAMENTATION, ARE ALSO TYPICAL OF SWEDISH STYLE. THE ORIENTAL DESIGNS ARE A FORM OF IMPORTED PATTERN THAT HAVE ALSO BECOME VERY MUCH PART OF THE SWEDISH-STYLE INTERIOR. (FOR MORE DETAILS ON CREATING A SWEDISH-STYLE ROOM, TURN TO SCANDINVAVIAN STYLE, IN PART THREE OF THIS BOOK, PAGE 184.)

Using this as a guide, you can mix patterns from the same family. For your first attempt at pattern-mixing, opt for checks and stripes. These can be used successfully as the only type of pattern within a room, or using the guidelines given above, various styles of this pattern can be combined. For example, a large checked design, featuring mainly an open cream background with large squares of terracotta and lines of black, can be successfully mixed with a smaller scale, two-colour check in black and cream. This can be further enhanced by a third design of terracotta featuring mid-sized black squares. This sort of pattern combination would work successfully within a room if partnered with textural-style fabrics and wallcoverings, or could be further developed into a room scheme that also featured a number of striped fabric designs. The key thing to remember is that you are mixing patterns which are each of a different scale.

Florals can also be effectively used together within a room. Choose a large densely patterned floral fabric and combine it with a very open, flowing, floral design in a complementary colourway. In addition, small bud designs, uniformly repeated in a geometric manner, will also work within the same room as the previous designs. Stripes and checks can then be added as they work universally with other pattern styles.

Above right: THIS CLASSICALLY INSPIRED BATHROOM IS A HAVEN OF PEACE. THE SCARCITY OF PATTERN ENSURES A CALMING AND RESTFUL ATMOSPHERE, BUT THE MONOGRAMS USED PLAY AN IMPORTANT PART IN THE FINISHED ROOM, BRINGING DETAIL AND INTEREST TO THE ROOM, DESPITE THEIR MINIMAL SIZE.

Using Geometric Pattern

Left: GEOMETRIC PATTERN ADDS ORDERED DETAIL TO A ROOM AND WILL WORK IN A NUMBER OF HISTORICALLY AND REGIONALLY STYLED SETTINGS. THIS STUNNING LIVING ROOM FEATURES TWO CHECKED DESIGNS OF VARYING SCALE IN THE SAME COLOURWAY, ONE ON THE RUG AND THE OTHER ON THE CHAIRS. THE COMBINATION OF BLACK AND YELLOW IS TAKEN FROM THE CLASSICAL PALETTE, YET THE ROOM IS MODERN AND ORIGINAL.

Right: THIS BRIGHT CONTEMPORARY DINING ROOM USES STRIKING GEOMETRIC PATTERN TO ADD IMPACT TO ITS BOLD COLOUR SCHEME. NOTICE HOW THE TWO COLOURS HAVE BEEN REPEATED IN THE SOFTER MOTIF PATTERN ON THE ADJACENT PART OF THE ROOM TO LINK THE TWO AREAS.

The term geometric pattern refers to checks, stripes, lattices and trellises. They are a very versatile tool for the interior designer, as their ordered manner allows them to be combined easily and effectively with other pattern types. They also have strong links with various historical and regional styles, such as the Victorian era and Scandinavian style, which makes them useful for injecting a sense of those interiors into a room.

Geometric pattern is ideal when compiling a scheme that has a masculine edge. This does not mean, however, that all geometric designs are unfeminine. Some very pretty and delicate patterns are geometric, and feature colours that have a strong feminine character. What most geometric patterns share is a sense of formality and order, which makes them perfect for smarter rooms or where a crisp contrast is needed to avoid more whimsical patterning.

Stripes generally add height to the length or width of the item they adorn, depending on the way in which the stripes are lying on the wall or furniture. So if you want your walls to appear taller, accentuate their height with vertical stripes. Also, a sofa decorated in horizontal stripes will look longer than one which is not. The

width of the stripes you choose is important too. Broad stripes will make an item or surface appear smaller than narrow stripes. This is with the exception of natural single-coloured fabrics, where the striped pattern is woven into the fabric rather than being featured in a separate colour to the background. As in all patterns in this colourway, their ability to deceive the eye is considerably weakened by their lack of powerful contrast colour.

The history of geometric pattern

Understanding the history of geometric pattern will enable you to create authentic period-style interiors. You can also, most usefully, learn from the experience of the designers of the past which patterns can be effectively combined with geometric designs in a decorative scheme. For more tips on creating a particular style with the patterns you choose, turn to Part Three, Themed Decorating, page 158.

Geometric designs have been popular throughout history. The Medieval and Renaissance eras saw geometric pattern which included chevrons (v-shaped motifs, either stacked on top of each other, or strung together to make a zig-zag pattern). Vertical stripes in two or more colours became increasingly popular and featured various designs in varying sizes of stripe. Striped designs were also used as a background for other patterns during these periods, with floral designs or small motifs worked on to them.

In the early eighteenth century, when French Empire, English Regency and American Federal styles of interior were fashionable, early Rococo-style fabrics featured trellis and lattice work designs, while geometric wallpapers were also highly popular. Striped fabrics and wallcoverings consisted of solid vertical bands of stripes, of varying widths and colours. Some featured small rows of scrolled decoration or foliage design. Classical-style Greek key borders and oriental-inspired lattice and trellis work were also widely seen, with Sweden, in particular, favouring trellis designs made up of foliage pattern.

In the second half of the eighteenth century, technical advances saw the introduction of more complex stripes. These were favoured by the advocates of neo-classical interiors. Chevrons were combined with stripes and the stripes were designed from leaves, urns and classical motifs, creating Etruscan-style fabrics and wallcoverings. Multicoloured woven checks featuring classical or floral embellishments were also widely used during this period.

With the end of the eighteenth century came the invention of a new fabric designed for bedding. Originally woven to keep feathers in and creepy crawlies out, ticking was a herringbone weave featuring a single-coloured stripe. This dark red and cream, blue and cream or beige and cream fabric is still popular. Now though, it is not only used as a bedding material, but for soft furnishings throughout the home, usually in rooms where a more informal finish is called for.

Regency stripes, as we now call them, first appeared in the early nineteenth century, or Regency period. Inspired by the striped bunting hung from the exterior of French public buildings to celebrate Napoleon's victory, these fabrics soon found their way into people's homes in the bold Chinese colours (see Part Three, Oriental Style, page 215) favoured at this time.

The early nineteenth century also saw twill-weave tartans in interiors, both in Britain and America. Stripes remained a favourite until the 1830s, but the wide range of checked fabrics being produced began to replace them in popularity. Printed ginghams, often imported from the east, were also very fashionable. These were colourful but not always colour-fast.

During the second half of the nineteenth century, many designs were influenced by a publication written by Owen Jones, *Grammar of Ornament* (1856), which stated that all ornament should be based on geometric

Above left: GEOMETRIC PATTERNS CAN LOOK EXTREMELY INTERESTING WHEN COVERING A PIECE OF FURNITURE DESIGNED WITH A NON-GEOMETRIC FORM. THIS SMALL CHAIR, FOR INSTANCE, HAS A FLOWER-SHAPED BACKREST WHICH IS ENHANCED BY A CONTRASTING GEOMETRIC UPHOLSTERY FABRIC.

Above right: THIS HOME OFFICE HAS USED LARGE BLOCKS OF NEUTRAL COLOUR TO ADD INTEREST AND PATTERN IN AN ORDERED MANNER, PERFECT FOR A STUDY AREA. WHILE STRONG IN ITS VISUAL IMPACT, THE COLOURS AND PATTERN USED ENSURE THAT THE INTERIOR IS FAR FROM FUSSY AND OVERBEARING.

construction. This had a great effect on the new Arts and Crafts and Aesthetic movements in Britain. This new way of thinking led to geometric pattern being used as a background to oriental and medieval motifs such as the pomegranate and the fleur de lys.

As we entered the twentieth century, geometric designs became particularly fashionable once again. The Art Deco period saw the development of wall-coverings featuring geometric pattern in the form of overlapping squares or triangles. Triangle designs were also popular in fabrics, as were patterns including chevrons and Aztec-inspired shapes.

Many historical geometric patterns have continued to be popular right up to the present day, with more irregular and abstract designs introduced in the Fifities and Sixties – all printed in the bright colours that are now so symbolic of those times.

Today, the emphasis has shifted from the colours used in the patterns to the texture of the fabric itself. Geometric patterns continue to be popular, but innovative weaving techniques have allowed the patterns to become an inherent yet distinctive part of the fabric, so that subtle, neutral colour schemes now have a higher profile than ever before.

Using Floral Pattern

Floral motifs have been a source of inspiration for fabric and wallpaper designers for centuries. Whether woven or printed, their natural ability to bring gentle detail and colour into the home has made them a popular choice for the interior designer and home decorator alike.

The range of floral motifs available is so wide and varying that you can use them to create any sort of look, from a small rustic cottage to a traditional country house or even a smart city apartment. To make your initial choice easier, and your final scheme more coherent, decide what sort of look you want to achieve, rather than simply looking for florals of any kind. Large floral motifs are used widely to create the country house style, often teamed with small repeat floral patterns; faded floral designs depicting wild roses will suit a cottage interior; or, for a Swedish look, opt for swags of handpainted flowers in panels or borders and combined with stripes and checks. If you do wish to create a regional or historical style, refer to the specific section in Part Three, Themed Decorating, page 158.

The scale and style of the pattern is as important as ever – especially if you are considering floral pattern for wallcoverings. Choose small buds for the walls of a tiny bedroom, sharp bright daisies for a more contemporary room, and large blooming flowers in soft shades for a grand effect in a generously proportioned space. If you cannot resist a large printed fabric and your room is on the small side, then restrict its use to the window with a blind or some curtains, and combine it with plain walls to balance the look.

Many floral motifs have a busying effect on a decorative scheme. In most cases this is enhanced and can be used as a feature. But if the colour scheme is in danger of becoming overbearing, stripes and checks of various proportions can be introduced to calm it down. If you want to mix florals with other florals, however, ensure that the complementary design is of a different scale to your dominant pattern, and that it is used in a smaller quantity than the main design. As long as you follow these guidelines, your mixing and matching should be successful, and will result in a creative and professional-looking layered effect.

The history of floral pattern

Throughout history floral designs have evolved and their styles changed. This is partly due to an increase in botanical reference material and also the changes in weaving and printing techniques. It is important to be familiar with these changes if you wish to decorate your

Above: THIS BEAUTIFUL COLLECTION OF GARDEN FLOWERS SITS PERFECTLY AGAINST A SMALL FLOWER MOTIF WALLPAPER. A LARGE-PATTERNED FABRIC FEATURING BOUQUETS OR VASES OF FLOWERS WOULD ALSO COMPLEMENT THE WALLPAPER IN THE SAME WAY.

Right: A TYPICAL SCANDINAVIAN FLORAL PATTERN IS A FLOWING STRIPE INCORPORATING SINGLE-COLOURED FLORAL MOTIFS, SUCH AS THESE TWO RED AND BLUE-GREY WALLCOVERINGS. HERE THEY ARE THE MAIN ELEMENT CREATING THE SCANDINAVIAN LOOK.

Above: USE OLD-FASHIONED FLORAL PRINTS TO COVER UPHOLSTERED FURNITURE IN A TRADITIONAL ROOM. THE YELLOW-BASED FLORAL FABRIC ON THIS COMFORTABLE CHAIR SITS WELL AGAINST THE RED-PAINTED WALL BEHIND, THANKS TO THE RED DETAIL WITHIN THE PATTERN. BOTH THE PAINT COLOUR AND THE PATTERN HAVE HISTORICAL CONNOTATIONS THAT SERVE TO FIX THIS ROOM IN A PERIOD STYLE.

Right: HERE THREE PATTERNS COMBINE, DEMONSTRATING THE IMPORTANCE OF A VARIATION IN THE SCALE AND DENSITY OF YOUR CHOSEN DESIGNS. A LARGE OPEN BACKGROUND FLORAL IS USED FOR SCATTER CUSHIONS, WHILE A FLOWING DESIGN WITH A MORE DENSE BACKGROUND IS USED ON THE CURTAINING. BOTH OF THESE FLORAL PATTERNS WORK EXTREMELY WELL WITH THE CHEVRON-DESIGNED GEOMETRIC UPHOLSTERY FABRIC. THE TWO-COLOURED STRIPE AT THE HEAD OF THE CURTAINING COMPLETES THE ROOM WITH A VERY PROFESSIONAL TOUCH.

home in a pure historical style. However, the current trend in more personal home-styling is leaving the door wide open to the mixing of various different period fabrics and patterns.

Prior to the seventeenth century, most fabrics and wallcoverings in Britain featured stylized flowers, with very symmetrical designs. It was only when knowledge of plant form grew and became more fashionable, as more source material became available, that floral designs became more realistic.

During the early eighteenth century, fabric and wallpaper designs became influenced by the surge in travel around the world, and by imports from the Orient. Unfamiliar flowers such as the chrysanthemum had begun to appear and this started a fashion for the more exotic. However, towards the end of the century, floral designs moved on again, away from the oriental designs to simpler floral motifs, such as poppies, daisies, and many styles of rose, along with other wild flowers. This offered the home decorator a range of refreshing and realistic country-style floral patterns.

Throughout the nineteenth century these naturally depicted floral designs remained popular. However, some formal, stylized designs were also produced in glazed cotton fabrics, which were developed within the Art Deco era in the early part of the twentieth century. Technological developments lead to more vivid colours being used in the printing and weaving of these designs, often with a more three-dimensional edge. The late twentieth century brought with it a revival of the Victorian, full-blown naturalistic floral design. So great was the demand for archive material that manufacturers began reproducing nineteenth century designs in great volume, and companies specializing in those styles, such as Laura Ashley, literally blossomed in the Eighties.

Now you can pick and mix from the floral designs of the past and the more contemporary designs. Much more recently, designers such as Tricia Guild began combining natural and stylized florals in bright vivid colourways, which signalled the start of a brave new approach to using colour in the home. For those of you who still prefer a muted approach to home-styling, there are plenty of contemporary designers who once again favour more simplistic and natural floral motifs. Colours here span the natural through to the bright, but are this time delivered in a more delicate and simplistic manner.

Using Motif Pattern

Motif patterns fall into two categories: representational and abstract. Representational designs are normally derived from nature – such as plants, animals, shells, flowers, the stars, moon and sun. Abstract or figurative motif patterns, on the other hand, include geometrically formed shapes such as polka dots, lozenges and Vitruvian scrolls. Every style of motif has its own individual character, making it easy to add personality or a sense of history to a room.

Left: GOTHIC-STYLE MOTIFS HAVE COME IN AND OUT OF FASHION AT VARIOUS TIMES THROUGHOUT HISTORY. ALTHOUGH IT IS NORMALLY CONSIDERED A RATHER HEAVY STYLE, ASSOCIATED WITH DARK WOOD FURNITURE, THIS LIVING ROOM SHOWS THAT GOTHIC STYLE CAN BE GIVEN A LIGHTER, AIRIER TREATMENT. THE MOTIF-COVERED WALLS ARE A DRAMATIC BUT NOT OVERPOWERING COMPLEMENT TO THE ARCH-SHAPED PELMET, CHAIRS, BOOKSHELVES AND DECORATED MIRROR.

Right: NOVICE OR CAUTIOUS DESIGNERS WILL FIND IT EASIER TO USE MOTIFS AROUND THE ROOM IF THE SCALE OF THE PATTERN IS VARIED. HERE, HOWEVER, THE SAME SIZE OF MOTIF HAS BEEN USED TO STUNNING EFFECT ON BOTH THE WALLS AND CURTAINING. THE NEUTRAL COLOUR SCHEME ENSURES THAT THE OVERALL DESIGN IS STYLISH AND NOT TOO OVERPOWERING.

Motifs can be used widely around a room, decorating anything from your fabrics and wallcoverings to objet d'art, flooring and lighting. You might be lucky enough to find a fabric decorated in a motif that appeals to you, and complementary accessories graced with the same design. If you cannot find the right accessories, or if you would prefer to start from scratch, you could stencil or stamp a motif on to the walls, and even on to fabrics and lampshades, using a fabric paint.

Motif pattern can be used to introduce a theme to a room. Bathrooms, in particular, suit the use of a repeat motif within a theme such as maritime. Plain walls develop greater character once stamped or stencilled with a shoal of fish, for instance, or maybe the occasional yacht. By stamping the same design in a smaller or larger scale on the bath panel or blind, the various elements of the room become linked and the theme becomes apparent. The motif should not be relied on as the only link within the scheme, however. Despite its ability to add a unifying strength to the room, it must be combined with a well planned colour scheme for a well balanced and aesthetically pleasing room.

The history of motif pattern

Motif patterns come and go throughout history as fashions emerge, go out of favour and are then revived again. The nineteenth century in particular saw plenty of revivals of historical motifs, but even today certain well used designs have been re-invented. If you want an interior that is historically accurate, you should try and explore as many source books as you can at the library – otherwise you may be committing a design faux-pas if you mix and match motifs from over the centuries, using only the colourways to link them. Here, for your inspiration, are some of the many motifs that have stood the test of time.

The Palladian interiors of the early eighteenth century featured many motif patterns. Classically inspired ornamentation such as dolphins, eagles, Roman and Greek masks were all popular at the time, while the favoured Rococo-style motifs were based on chinoiserie

birds (a western interpretation of oriental style), scroll work, French-inspired pictorial motifs and lanterns.

Later in the eighteenth century you could see combinations of rosettes, Roman motifs, urns, vases and scroll work foliage. These were all an integral part of British Adam-style, neo-classical and American Federal-style interiors. Gothic revivalists, however, used portraiture, featuring clerks and masons at work, and motif designs inspired by flora and fauna for their decorative interiors at the end of the century.

Classical interiors during the early part of the nineteenth century also featured motifs. Etruscan designs, Greek in origin, such as palmettes, vases, winged lions, eagles, festoons and medallions were all popular, as well as Roman-style designs, including olive wreaths, rosettes, griffins and winged touches. These emblems were popular across Europe and America. France, in particular, identified itself with the use of Roman-style motif, largely due to Napoleon's desire for his country to be associated with the power and strength of the Roman Empire. Egyptian designs, such as sphinxes, lotus flowers and scarabs, were also featured during this period. When recreating a classical interior, look to using these motifs in both fabric and wallpaper designs. Trompe l'oeil borders depicting various classical motifs are an effective and authentic way of adding historical motif patterns. Turn to Classical Style in Part Three, page 174 for more suggestions for creating this look.

The mid-nineteenth century saw a battle between two architectural styles – Gothic revival and classical. The motifs associated with these styles were therefore both very much in vogue, and can still be seen, successfully used side by side, today. Try combining the fleur de lys, scrolling leaves, and general heraldic motifs with the traditional classical motifs, such as the urn, and neither will look out of place.

If your tastes tend towards the more colourful or exotic, let yourself be inspired by the mid-nineteenth century interest in Indian-style designs. These included paisley patterns based on designs originating in India, and Moorish designs, such as the arabesque.

Contemporary styles at the end of the nineteenth century covered a wide range of design themes. Europe and America were subjected to a mix of revivalist styles, including Gothic, Rococo and Pompeiian. These decorative styles made way at the beginning of the twentieth century, however, for a new trend in interiors and also architecture, based on the principles of the Arts and Crafts and Aesthetic movements. Motifs were a prominent feature of these new trends. For example, Arts and Crafts wallpapers featured stylized repeated natural forms interwoven with medieval motifs, while the Aesthetic and Art Nouveau movement favoured oriental-style birds, insect motifs, flowers (especially sunflowers) and scroll work.

The early part of the twentieth century, especially the Thirties, saw the revival of certain styles of motif to enhance Art Deco interiors: Egyptian and Aztec designs, such as scarabs, stepped shapes and sun motifs, were seen gracing walls, ceramics and furniture.

These were, however, soon replaced by more geometric and abstract designs. This sort of patterning continued to be popular until the Fifties, when motifs inspired by scientific discoveries (particularly in space) took America and Britain by storm, accompanied by stylized motifs of fruit, such as apples and pears.

The Sixties saw the emergence of motifs set against a geometric background. Designs in America, in particular, displayed large tropical leaves and flowers, fruit and vegetables, together with motifs derived from kitchen paraphernalia such as the wine bottle and coffee pot.

Today, motifs are as popular as ever, most based on images revived from the past, but given a fresh treatment with lively, bright colour. However, the recent popularization of the neutral colour scheme, as well as the even more recent introduction of metallic paints, have enabled popular motif designs to be used across an even broader spectrum of colour and texture than ever before.

Using Pictorial Pattern

Pictorial patterns are ideal for developing a specific theme or atmosphere
in a room, adding either a historical or a regional touch to walls or fabrics.
Humans have been using pictorial representations to decorate their homes
since the time of the first cave dwellers, with historical events or more
mundane day-to-day life inspiring designers throughout history.

Above: PICTORIAL DESIGNS ARE A GOOD CHOICE FOR
CHILDREN'S BEDROOMS, ALLOWING YOU TO CREATE A THEMED
WONDERLAND FOR YOUR CHILD IF YOU ARE ON A TIGHT BUDGET,
IT IS BEST TO RESTRICT YOUR USE OF STRONGLY THEMED
PICTORIAL PATTERN TO ITEMS THAT YOU CAN AFFORD TO
REPLACE EASILY, SUCH AS A WALLPAPER BORDER OR A DUVET
COVER. YOU CAN GUARANTEE THAT A DESIGN THAT IS POPULAR
WITH YOUR CHILD TODAY WILL SOON BE OUTGROWN.

Examine the styles of most historical periods and
you will discover some form of pictorial pattern.
From medieval tapestries depicting great feats of heroic
achievement to the eighteenth-century toile de Jouy
portraying romantic scenes of rural life, they all capture
the political and cultural climate in which the designer
of the time lived.

Some pictorial pattern could equally come under the
heading of motif pattern (see Using Motif Pattern, page
54). Animals, classical urns, plants and birds can all be
found under this heading, but may also fall into the
motif pattern category. Pictorial pattern, however, is
more scenic than a motif design which can stand inde-
pendently. In pictorial pattern, the individual motifs are
purely one element of a more complex picture.

As with all forms of pattern, pictorial designs are
subject to the influences of architecture and the fashions of interior style at any given period. However, one
thing remains true of pictorial pattern – its constant
ability to introduce a specific style or theme to a decorative scheme. Simply by decorating your walls or
windows with a pictorial wallcovering or fabric you will
anchor your room in a particular era, country or film
set, be it rural eighteenth-century England, mythical
China or Disneyland.

If you want to start cautiously with pictorial design,
then introduce it on cushion covers, a blind or perhaps
a lampshade. Curtaining is not for the unadventurous,
as once closed at night pictorially patterned curtains
will make a dramatic impact on a room. Covering your
walls with a pictorial pattern should not be undertaken
lightly, although it can look stunning in the right setting. Remember the importance of scale, and refer to
the tips in The Basic Principles of Using Pattern, page
40, before investing in rolls of wallpaper. You could
start by buying one roll, or ask for a large sample, and

Left: GRECIAN- OR ROMAN-INSPIRED PICTORIAL DESIGNS CAN BE USED TO GREAT EFFECT IN A CLASSICAL SETTING. THIS KITCHEN FEATURES URN DESIGNS IN A MONOCHROMATIC COLOURED FABRIC, COMBINED WITH STRONG STRIPES IN THE SAME COLOURWAY. THIS CREATES A STYLISH LOOK WHICH IS RATHER MORE ORIGINAL THAN THE OBVIOUS KITCHENWARE PATTERNS. THE PATTERNED CURTAINS ALSO HELP TO ADD A SENSE OF DRAMA TO THE EATING AREA WHEN THEY ARE CLOSED IN THE EVENING.

then tack it to the walls, preferably in two lengths. This will give you a good impression of the effect that your chosen wallpaper will have on the space.

In some rooms you can afford to be daring with pictorial pattern and go for maximum impact. Bathrooms and children's bedrooms are ideal places to introduce large-scale imaginative scenes, be it with stencils or even a mural. Turn to the sections on pictorial pattern in Children's Room Style, page 116 and Bathroom Style, page 130 in Part Two for more inspiration.

The history of pictorial pattern

During medieval times, wallhangings, mainly in the form of tapestries, depicted the history of the period. Ecclesiastical scenes, battles, tournaments and hunting parties were all highly fashionable. Pictorial wallhangings remained popular during the Renaissance and through to the French and English Baroque periods, by which time the designs had become very complex, using sophisticated techniques and realistic colour.

Right: THERE IS A WIDE RANGE OF WHAT ARE KNOWN AS 'WHIMSICAL' PICTORIAL PATTERNS AVAILABLE. HERE WE SEE TOPIARY-INSPIRED FIGURES FEATURED ON A STUNNING WALLPAPER WHICH WOULD ADD HUMOUR AND STYLE TO ANY ROOM.

Rococo style, in the early eighteenth century, introduced a less formal type of pictorial pattern. It was often frivolous and extremely colourful, with silk, cotton and tapestry hangings featuring oriental-style designs and Arabian or Moorish landscapes. The expansion of trade overseas fuelled a fashion in pictorial designs featuring foreign travel and native people. Scenes depicted included figures taking tea or playing musical instruments.

Towards the middle of the eighteenth century, tapestry wallhangings became less popular and more delicate images of the English or French countryside became the inspiration for many designs, although chinoiserie designs for fabric and wallpaper remained popular throughout the eighteenth century. Printed, cotton fabric, known as toile de Jouy, was being produced in the

Jouy factory in France. Their most popular pictorial design was oriental scenes, although romantic representations of rural life were also featured. These designs remained popular in the United States and Europe well into the nineteenth century. The fashion conscious of the time also used printed interpretations of Greco-Roman statues and architecture. Even paintings by Titian and Tintoretto were printed on to wallcoverings for a truly opulent look.

Panoramic wallpapers became fashionable at the end of the eighteenth-century period. Rather like murals, these exceptionally large designs displayed detailed scenes of the exploration of the South Pacific and the French Revolution as well as views of various European and American cities. In neo-classical interiors the idea was developed into printed, trompe l'oeil designs,

Left: THIS STYLISH FABRIC, FEATURING PICTORIAL REPRESENTATIONS OF BIRDS' EGGS AND FEATHERS, MAKES A REFRESHING ALTERNATIVE TO TRADITIONAL FLORAL OR MOTIF PATTERNS. THE CALLIGRAPHY-DECORATED WALLPAPER MAKES AN IDEALLY SUBTLE BACKDROP, WHICH BOTH COMPLEMENTS THE CHAIR AND ALLOWS IT TO REMAIN A PROMINENT FEATURE.

which featured festooned fabrics and gilded ornamentation, together with classical Greek designs.

Like other styles of pattern, certain pictorial designs would experience an ebb and flow in popularity. Classical revivals, for example, were frequent all around the world, while Gothic revivals occurred mainly in Britain, but both these designs continued to be popular for wallcoverings and textiles, right through to the turn of the century. A range of sentimental designs were also being used. These were multicoloured pictorial patterns depicting pets, railways trains and little children, which were mass-produced and found their way into the decoration of many ordinary family homes.

Pictorial designs took a refreshing turn at the beginning of the twentieth century when Art Nouveau designers introduced elegant figures and elongated plant designs. The Arts and Crafts movement, however, from the end of the nineteenth century preferred medieval-style designs featuring human forms set against floral backgrounds.

Early twentieth-century Art Deco and modernist designers rarely used pictorial fabrics or wallcoverings. However, pictorial designs experienced a revival during the later twentieth century. Toile de Jouy fabrics and wallpapers, classical designs featuring urns and statues, and medieval ranges have all been popular at some point in this century. A resurgence in the craft of découpage in recent years has brought more pictorial pattern into more people's homes than had been seen previously, with many people decorating small pieces of furniture if not creating a complete eighteenth-century-style printed room.

CREATING
decorative schemes

To successfully complete a decorative scheme you need to ensure that all the various elements of the room will work in unison – combining pattern with texture and colour in such a way that a sense of balance is achieved and no one piece is allowed to dominate the room at the expense of the others.

Remember to consider every aspect of your room carefully. A beautifully designed room should not rely on one specific element for success. The best decorative schemes should gain compliments such as 'What a wonderful room', rather than 'What a great pair of curtains'.

Start with a definite brief, listing your practical and aesthetic requirements for that space. Relaxing interiors benefit from the use of gentle pattern and cool colours. Stimulating schemes, however, rely on vibrant colour and lively pattern. Do not commit yourself to any one element until you have combined it with the additional items required to produce a complete scheme. You may find a fabric for curtaining, for example, but be unable to team it with a complementary upholstery fabric that allows you to fulfil your design brief. This can result in a room that is pleasing but not exactly what you were hoping for.

The best way of seeing whether or not the different elements of a room will work well together is to combine all the various samples you are considering on a board, in the same proportions as they would appear in the room. (In other words, the wallpaper sample should be much larger than the armchair sample.) Overlap the samples as they would lie in your room, the armchair next to the curtains and so on, and play around with different combinations until you find a scheme that appeals to you.

Left: A MINIMAL BUT CLEVER USE OF COLOUR AND BEAUTIFULLY CRAFTED PIECES OF FURNITURE SET THE TONE FOR THIS MODERN INTERIOR. THE RICH WARM TONES USED EVOKE THE NATURAL PALETTE OF A FOREIGN CLIMATE, WHILE THE BASIC CHAIR STYLE ALSO SUGGESTS AN ETHNIC INFLUENCE.

Single-colour Schemes

**The single-colour or monochromatic scheme is based on tones of just one colour –
so its success is reliant on a carefully planned mix of tonal variation and texture.**

When lacking experience in colour-scheming, people tend to 'match' colours too exactly, hanging curtains that are the same tone and colour as the sofa, and adding cushions the same colour as the walls. This results in a flat and uninteresting room. Imagine your room as a photograph. If it was printed in black and white with no tonal variation, the resulting picture would have no depth, definition or interest. Remember this when working on a monochromatic scheme in your home – it will be very dull if it is created using just one shade and tone of a single colour. Instead, you should look to find fabrics and wallcoverings in different tones of the same colour, and with a variation of texture.

Once your sample board or room is nearly complete, you may decide that it would benefit from an accent colour to add impact to the scheme. In a room designed to be a relaxing haven, it may be wise to choose an accent colour that is harmonious (from the same side of the colour wheel), to avoid over-stimulating the eye. However, a room that will be used for more lively activities will benefit from a contrasting accent chosen from the opposite side of the wheel.

Above: THIS MODERN BATHROOM BENEFITS FROM A FEELING OF SPACE CREATED BY THE COOL SINGLE-COLOUR SCHEME. THE BLENDED BLUE MOSAIC TILES ADD TONAL VARIATION, ALLOWING THE PLAIN WALLS TO HIGHLIGHT THE INTERESTING SHAPE OF THE ROOM.

Left: TRADITIONAL TYPES OF ROOM CAN ALSO BENEFIT FROM THE WELL PLANNED MONOCHROMATIC COLOUR SCHEME.

Where to use a monochromatic scheme

- To provide an undemanding background to a central feature within a room. If you have a patterned sofa, for example, and either want to avoid mixing patterns or wish to make a feature of its style, then a monochromatic style of decorative background is ideal.

- A contemporary or minimalist setting will suit a single-colour scheme. It will act as a simple foil to modern pieces of furniture and decorative modern art. The most successful schemes will have ample tonal variation. Ensure you add some textural interest with fur fabrics, knitted textiles and bouclé weaves.

- A traditional room would be well served by a monochromatic scheme combined with traditional fabrics and antique pieces of furniture. Do not underestimate the power of decorative items such as paintings and accessories. Cushions and throws can introduce small amounts of pattern to a tonal scheme such as this, and the overall effect will then look decorative and far from austere.

- To increase the impression of space. A monochromatic scheme in a receding colour will supply a room with an expansive atmosphere, allowing you to use pattern in a bolder form on the central feature, such as the bed. Lighting will also help to create an illusion of space in this setting. Limit the lighting to the area around the bed, allowing the remainder of the room to fade into the darkness.

- A classically inspired room, in either a traditional or modern setting, will suit a monochromatic scheme in black and white – the 'non-colours'. Grey can also be introduced into this style of interior to add further depth to the scheme.

Choosing the colours for your decorative scheme

The colours you choose are crucial to the scheme – especially those that you select for your walls as they dominate such a large part of the room.

- Most of us have to create a scheme based around existing items. Look first at any piece which incorporates a number of colours in its design. It has done the colour-scheming for you. Pick out the key colours in the item and use them around the room – in the same proportions as they appear in your starting piece.

- We have learned that warm colours advance, while cool colours recede. You should use this knowledge to make an area appear larger or smaller or to make an individual wall look closer or further away. It is amazing how you can play with the perceived dimensions of a room in this way.

- Instead of fighting it, why not make a feature of a dark or small room? Choose warm, dark colours to create a dramatic and intimate environment and use candles or well positioned accent lights to add additional atmosphere.

- If you are unsure whether to choose a matt or silk finish, consider the quality of your wall surface. Use matt finish paints on uneven or flawed walls, as satin or gloss finishes will only highlight any problem areas.

- If you are thinking of using a dramatic colour for a room, take into consideration the fact that, once applied to the walls, the colour used will reflect off adjacent walls. Therefore, if you are covering all the surfaces in one colour, you should choose a shade that is slightly lighter than the one you like – the combined reflections of the lighter colour will help to achieve the shade you originally wanted.

- Be aware of the effect additional blocks of colour within the room might have on the walls. Pale green painted walls, for example, may take on a rosy glow if they are combined with a deep pink carpet.

- Avoid using bright white paint in period schemes. Today's paint has been artificially brightened and is quite unlike the white of the past, so instead use an off white, known to designers as 'dirty white', for an authentic style.

Contrasting Colour Schemes

Colour schemes that combine colours from opposite sides of the colour wheel are known as 'contrasting' or 'complementary' schemes. The scheme does not have to feature only the two chosen colours, as white and black can also be introduced.

Left: ORANGE AND BLUE ARE A LIVELY COMBINATION OF COLOURS AND HAVE BEEN USED TO GREAT EFFECT IN THIS STUNNING HALLWAY. NOTICE HOW ORANGE HAS BEEN ALLOWED TO DOMINATE THE SCHEME, WITH THE BLUE BEING USED ONLY TO CONTRAST AND HIGHLIGHT CERTAIN FEATURES.

Right: CONTRASTING COLOURWAYS ARE NOT LIMITED TO THE MORE CONTEMPORARY STYLE OF INTERIOR DESIGN. HERE RED IS USED TO ADD LIFE AND DEFINITION TO THE YELLOW WALLCOVERING AND FABRIC IN WHAT IS UNMISTAKABLY A TRADITIONAL ENVIRONMENT.

Vibrant and lively, contrasting schemes give a room life and vitality and are ideal for stimulating rooms, or rooms that are used for shorter periods of time. However, they need not be overpowering, as a successful contrasting combination should not feature colours used in an equal proportion. When contrasting or complementary colours combine, they act to make each individual colour more powerful, so allow one colour to dominate. For example, you should avoid covering your walls and floor in contrasting colours, as they both cover so much area. Instead, use the contrasting colour in smaller splashes around the room.

If, however, your room has already evolved with equal quantities of contrasting colours, it may be rescued by the use of an additional third colour as an accent. Use accents with caution, as you wish it purely to act as a seasoning rather than becoming one of the main ingredients in the room.

Places to consider using a contrasting scheme would include children's bedrooms, where the strong contrasts offer the perfect background for colourful toys, or a vibrant sitting room for a young couple who enjoy entertaining.

Colour suggestions for contrasting schemes

Many fabric designers produce fabrics combining contrasting colours, so why not take such a fabric as a starting point and use the colours, as combined by the designer, within the interior. It is the simplest way of producing a contrasting or complementary room design and the fabric can be used as a central feature within a room. Otherwise try the following combinations:

● **Red and green** are direct opposites on the colour wheel, making them the strongest of contrasting partners. To reduce this effect, tonal variation can be introduced to create a scheme comprising of green and pink or green and burgundy, for example. Or you could allow various shades of green to dominate and then add a little red for a more palatable finished scheme.

● **Blue and orange** are also strong contrasting partners which work wonderfully in contemporary-style interiors. Try introducing blocks of orange and blue into a framework made up mainly of white with touches of black.

● **Yellow and blue** is a popular foundation for a contrasting scheme, offering the balance of a warm and cool colour. Do not limit them to use in their original primary form, however, as the addition of shade, tone and tint will broaden your choice of colour selection.

● **Red and yellow** in their richest shades work well as a combination in traditional interiors. Combined with a mixture of checked and floral fabrics, they produce a warm and welcoming room.

Harmonious Colour Schemes

If you wish to create a colourful, yet soothing, colour scheme, a harmonious combination could well be the perfect solution. Produced by the combination of colours from just one side of the colour wheel, this decorative style is easy to live with and restful. So versatile is this type of scheme, in fact, that it is suitable for every room in the house and most, if not all, age groups.

Left: A HARMONIOUS BLEND OF BLUE, GREEN AND YELLOW COMBINE WITH GEOMETRIC PATTERNING TO PRODUCE AN INSPIRING MODERN INTERIOR THAT IS ALSO RESTFUL AND EASY ON THE EYE. YOU SHOULD NOTE, HOWEVER, THAT BOTH THE FABRIC DESIGNER AND THE ROOM DESIGNER HAVE INTRODUCED SOME SMALL BLOCKS OF CONTRASTING COLOUR TOO. VIOLET AND SOFT PURPLE IS TO BE SEEN IN THE DISCREET FORM OF CANDLES ON THE WINDOW SILL AND IN A DELICATE REPEAT LEAF MOTIF ON THE CURTAIN FABRIC.

Right: HARMONIOUS COLOUR SCHEMES CAN BE WARM AND COSY OR COOL AND RELAXING, DEPENDING ON WHICH AREA OF THE COLOUR WHEEL YOU FOCUS ON FOR YOUR PALETTE. THIS BLEND OF VIOLET AND BLUE FROM THE COOLER SIDE OF THE COLOUR WHEEL CREATES A RESTFUL, STYLISH AND AIRY SITTING ROOM.

Blues and greens, pinks and violets, and yellows and oranges are all harmonious combinations. These partnerships do not limit you purely to two colours, of course. An understanding of the colour wheel will enable you to appreciate the variations available within each category. Violet-blue, blue and aquamarine can all combine to create this type of scheme, as can lavender blue, violet and pink.

This type of colour scheme does not fall into warm and cool colour categories alone, as the sections where these colours meet on the colour wheel can also be the basis of a successful scheme. Blue, green and yellow is a harmonious combination, as is red, orange and violet.

As well as creating a room which features harmonious colours on the walls and fabrics, however, think also to uniting a scheme with paintings and artwork. Individual blocks of colour can be combined in one dramatic painting or decorative wall hanging, turning what some might view as an afterthought or a luxury item into a successful unifying tool for the decorator.

Where to use a harmonious scheme

Harmonious colour schemes are a simple way of harnessing the powers associated with certain colour types to counteract the specific problems that are evident in your room, such as a lack of light or space.

- A small room will benefit from a harmonious scheme consisting of cool colours to give the room a spacious feel. It has already been explained how cool colours recede and this can be used to great effect in this environment.

- A large room designed for family relaxation will suit a harmonious scheme based around warm colours on the colour wheel. Pinks, reds and peaches will all give the room a cosy and welcoming appearance.

- In rooms where you want to make a feature of a patterned fabric, such as on a sofa, use blocks of individual harmonious colours from the pattern on various items of furniture or dress individual walls in plain colour. The patterned item then serves to unite the whole scheme successfully.

- In a room where you want to emphasize texture, rather than colour, a harmonious colour scheme will create a subtly coordinated backdrop for the textured items. A room decorated in plain blocks of colour needs the additional dimension supplied by contrasting tactile materials. This is currently a very fashionable approach to interior design and is used across a diverse range of decorative styles such as oriental and contemporary.

Neutral Colour Schemes

The neutral colour scheme has become very popular in recent years. Relaxing and textural, it has offered a new approach for the interior decorator and is a reaction against the bright, contrasting schemes that have previously been so popular.

A neutral type of colour scheme is produced by a combination of 'non-colours', such as white, grey and black, plus brown, beige and cream. Using these colours in isolation, with no hint of any brighter shade, produces a very natural look and a sense of calm.

A plain painted background of white or cream is stylish and practical, giving a room a spacious air – ideal for many modern properties which have smaller rooms. Do not be afraid that the finished effect will be uninteresting or bland. You can add deeper, natural colour in your furniture and furnishings without moving beyond the neutral spectrum.

If you have a small family and have always considered a neutral scheme completely impractical, then think again. Colours such as chocolate, coffee and caramel are especially popular currently, and offer the home decorator more serviceable colour than white or cream for use either as hardworking upholstery or purely as a striking contemporary element within a neutral scheme. Also, with the introduction of machine-washable textiles for upholstery and the wide range of stain-repelling finishes now available for soft furnishings, you can afford to be a bit braver than before with your choice of fabric colours.

Left: Using neutral colours within the home environment should not result in the production of uninspiring interiors. See how chocolate brown and off white are brought together in this wonderful living room to create a room that is modern and fresh, as well as relaxing.

Right: Neutral combinations work very well when carefully applied to a traditional setting. The lack of strong colour gives the room a timeless appeal – the perfect solution for anyone wanting to avoid being led by fashion or fad.

Adding interest to a neutral scheme

This type of scheme thrives on the addition of texture, especially when it complements the back-to-nature feel of the room, for instance stone, wood and fur. More contemporary-looking interiors can successfully add a touch of silver, pewter or stainless steel for a greater contrast. Here are some more suggestions:

● In a traditional setting, try adding natural carved timber or distressed pieces of furniture finished in non-colours, combined with beautifully sensuous furnishing fabrics, for a room full of tonal and textural variation.

● In a bedroom, use crisp white bed linen with caramel-coloured soft woollen blankets and a faux fur throw on a handpainted bed, for the ultimate in luxury and textural contrast.

● Give the room an oriental-inspired minimalist look (see Part Three, Oriental Style, page 214 for more details) and introduce textured woven fabrics, natural floor-coverings such as coir and seagrass, and natural timber venetian blinds.

● Add the latest in contemporary materials for a chic neutral look. The recent surge of woven and textural fabrics work particularly well in this setting, especially when combined with sheer fabrics, such as voile, at the window.

● The neutral scheme is an ideal setting for collections of interesting artefacts and paintings. Oriental and African tribal carvings and global pieces of art and furniture are now widely available and are greatly enhanced by a tonal, natural backdrop.

2

ROOM-BY-ROOM DECORATING

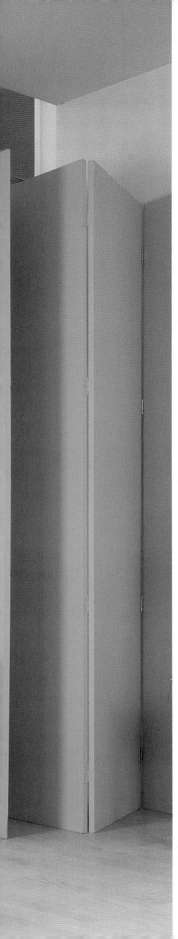

LIVING ROOM
style

The living room is often the first room in the house to receive design attention. An area often used both for family relaxation and formal entertaining, it's a room that has to be hardworking, practical, comfortable and aesthetically pleasing.

Colour and pattern, as we already know, can have a profound effect on the ambience of a room. Harnessing their powers can help to create an atmosphere reflective of your personality and preferred decorative style.

Consider the impression you want to give to the outside world, as the living room is probably the most public room in your home. You can have it warm and cosy, so that it is a welcoming friendly room, or cool and elegant – a sleek formal room designed to impress. You could choose a vibrant decorative style or a more refined one. But on top of this, colour and pattern can help you make the best use of the space available.

Not many people have the pleasure of beginning their decorative scheme from scratch. Most people have a starting point, such as a sofa or an inherited pair of curtains, that needs to be worked around. But even if you are one of the lucky few starting with a blank canvas, maximizing the effect of colour and pattern on a room is very empowering.

On the following pages we look at how colour and pattern can be used in living rooms of various different shapes and sizes to create an individual style and atmosphere.

Left: This chic living room manages to combine a style that is minimal and impressive with a laidback feeling of comfort.

Living Rooms/*Geometric*

The ordered manner in which a geometric pattern is designed gives it its unique quality. Geometric patterning can introduce detail to a room scheme, delivered either in a simple or smart, but always unfussy, manner. This is one of the joys of using geometric designs in interiors. Checks, stripes, lattices and trellis patterns can be used to tone down a busy floral living room or can add a sharp formality to a scheme.

When using geometric pattern in a living room, it is best to first determine what practical considerations need to be taken into account. Is the room purely for entertaining? In this case, any choice of geometric design could be used successfully within the scheme. If the room also has to withstand the rigours of a growing family, however, a range of geometric patterns in deep tones and colours can work together or individually to create a smart yet practical environment.

A sofa in a well used living room would give its owner years of service if it was upholstered in a woven check made up of practical blocks of colour. Many woven striped fabrics are also a practical solution for the multifunctional room. Not only do they offer a hard-wearing, spot-concealing surface, but they also have the benefit of adding a formal touch – ideal for a room used for entertaining as well as general family living. However, be careful of using fine designs, such as ticking. This style of traditional stripe, originally used to line pillows and mattresses, is now extremely popular for upholstery and soft furnishings, but it is very delicate and so better placed in rooms which are used less frequently.

Many find the thought of combining a selection of different patterns quite daunting, especially when they all come from the same pattern family. Most people would steer away from mixing tartans, for example, but it can be done with striking results. The sofa in the foreground of this Mediterranean-style living room (left) is a good example of pattern-mixing. Various geometric patterns sit happily together on this fine-striped sofa, linking the sofa with the overall room scheme, by echoing the gold of the walls and introducing a warm red. Gold and red is featured in all the cushion designs and this, coupled with the textural quality of the tapestry and woven fabrics used, creates an aesthetically pleasing collection of geometric patterns.

The floor of this stylized Mediterranean living room featured on the left is laid with rustic terracotta floor tiles in a geometric pattern, with contrasting coloured inserts. This provides a practical and stylish floorcovering on to which the mixture of antique and painted country furniture can sit easily.

Stripes can be used on the walls, as they are invaluable for adding height to rooms; walls covered with a design featuring a vertical stripe draw the eye upwards, which makes the ceiling appear higher. This is a useful device when decorating modern properties that tend not to have the height of more traditional dwellings.

Left: PEOPLE SHY AWAY FROM USING GEOMETRIC PATTERNS EXCLUSIVELY WITHIN A SCHEME, WORRIED THAT THE ROOM WILL APPEAR HARD AND AUSTERE. THIS WILL NOT BE THE CASE IF COLOUR IS CHOSEN CAREFULLY AND THE FABRICS ARE USED AGAINST A SOFT TEXTURAL BACKGROUND SUCH AS THE COLOURWASHED WALLS FEATURED IN THIS WONDERFUL ROOM.

Above: GINGHAM HAS ALWAYS BEEN A WELL LOVED FABRIC, AS IT HAS A FRESH AND WELCOMING QUALITY. IT CREATES A SIMPLE BUT LASTING LOOK, WHICH CAN BE BOTH TRADITIONAL AND CONTEMPORARY. HERE THE COMBINATION OF BLUE AND LILAC CHECKS IS PUNCTUATED BY A TOUCH OF SOFT LIME TO CREATE A FRESH AND RELAXING LIVING ROOM.

Living Rooms/*Floral*

From the living room of a country cottage to the parlour in the Victorian town house, floral designs have been used by home decorators the world over for centuries. It is no wonder then that this style of pattern is so often a preferred choice for many when decorating a living room.

Floral motifs, as with most patterns, offer a wide range of style and theme options. In fact, so vast is the range of floral material available, it is a good idea to give yourself a strict design brief before you go shopping to narrow down your options and make your final choice of design and pattern easier.

If you have a great love of all things floral, but want to create a simple and elegant living room, introduce floral pattern to the room in a reserved manner. A rug featuring flowers in a subtle colourway, and a formal chair upholstered in an Adams-style print with scrolls and flowers, would be the perfect way of quietly introducing some floral imagery to an otherwise classical room.

Floral fabrics can bring a faded, antiquated elegance to a room, transporting the inhabitants to times past. Alternatively, they can introduce a vibrant modern freshness to a room, delivering the colours and patterns associated with a summer garden into our very homes. The living room seen here (main picture) features a stunning floral sofa which has been combined with very simple, clean lines for the curtaining and other upholstery to retain an open and uncluttered atmosphere. This approach ensures the finished room has a very modern feel, despite being in a traditional setting.

It is true to say that with many floral patterns it is the way the fabric is used, as much as the fabric design itself, that influences the final effect. A floral fabric, teamed with a complementary small-scale floral motif and made into very elaborate frilled and ruched soft furnishings, would take on a totally different character from the same fabric used with a stripe in a pair of simple curtains. Stripes, country plaids and checks sober a floral scheme, adding detail while supplying an ordered edge to the room.

If you are opting for a floral scheme for your furniture and curtains, be quite cautious with your choice of flooring. The current trend in country-style interiors takes a more reserved approach than the more flowery traditional cottage look which layered florals upon florals. Floral pattern still has a very important part to play, but it is now set against a simpler background of colourwashed or plain walls, with traditional stone or timber flooring.

Left: TRADITIONAL ARCHITECTURE AND FLORAL PATTERNING DOES NOT HAVE TO ADD UP TO A BUSY TRADITIONAL ENVIRONMENT. FLORAL FABRICS ARE GIVEN A VERY MODERN FEEL BY COMBINING THEM WITH STRIPES THROUGHOUT THIS SIMPLY STYLED LIVING ROOM.

Above: COUNTRY COTTAGE INTERIORS ARE ALWAYS RELAXED AND WELCOMING AND MAKE AN IDEAL ATMOSPHERE FOR A FAMILY LIVING ROOM. IN THIS ROOM, FLORAL PATTERNING COMBINES WITH CHECKS AND STRIPES TO CREATE AN ORDERED COUNTRY COTTAGE-STYLE ROOM.

Living Rooms/*Motif*

Motif designs fall, in the main, into two categories: figurative (that is
geometrically based forms, including lozenges, polka dots, Greek keys and
scrolls) and representational. The latter is derived from living things, shells,
stars, flowers and the fleur de lys. These patterns offer the home decorator
an unimaginable range of design options.

Left: THE STAR MOTIF WALLPAPER FEATURED IN THIS LIVING ROOM IS THE PERFECT BACKGROUND FOR THE GILT SCONCES, MIRROR AND PENDANT LIGHT, GIVING THE ROOM ITS OPULENT FEEL. STAR MOTIFS CAN BE USED TO EMBELLISH WALLCOVERINGS, FABRICS, LAMPSHADES, AND EVEN CEILINGS. GOLD STARS ON A RED BASE MAKE A REGAL STATEMENT, WHILE GOLD ON DEEP BLUE IS REMINISCENT OF THE NATIVITY, CREATING THE ILLUSION OF AN EXPANSIVE DARK SKY ILLUMINATED BY THE STARS.

Left: HERE BRAVE USE OF A REPRESENTATIONAL MOTIF HAS TRANSFORMED A BLANK ROOM INTO SOMETHING SPECIAL. STENCILLED URNS DECORATE LIGHTLY WASHED WALLS IN THE LIVING AREA OF THIS ROOM WHILE CONTINUING THIS THEME WITH THE CLASSICAL BLACK BALUSTRADING LINKS THE RAISED DINING AREA TO THE REST OF THE ROOM.

In the living room the motif can be used to unify your scheme, give it a theme and add a little of your personality to a room. There is such a wide range of motifs to choose from, each having a unique character. The fleur de lys, for example, adds a traditional strength to the most modern of colour schemes, and stars and moons are great fun, but also have a mystical quality. The Greek key and urn motif provides a very classical and elegant reserve to a room.

A motif is the perfect way of tying together elements within a living room scheme by using it as a recurring theme, appearing on various surfaces within the room. This type of approach is also reliant on colour. It is not possible to rely purely on the motif to draw the items together; the motif must also fall into a well planned colour scheme. In a carefully considered room, the finished effect is stunning, especially when the scale of the motif, and the distance between each motif, varies from item to item.

There are a number of ways to use a motif in a living room. One option is to use it as a patterned backdrop to plain furniture and furnishings. This might be a motif-covered wallpaper, or the motif could be applied to a surface by the use of a stencil or rubber stamp. By applying the motif yourself, you are free to create the exact background you require. You may only wish to create a border of the motif around the picture rail or cornicing. This is the ideal way of linking a motif used in a furnishing fabric with the rest of the room's scheme. Alternatively, you may wish to add extra height to the room by repeating the motif in a vertical stripe down the walls.

Stencils and stamps can also be used on your living room floor to add some decorative detail. Using the correct paints or stains, you can add your chosen motif to floorboards, coir matting and rugs. This offers a very practical and stylish floor finish in a busy family room.

There is an enormous range of motif-covered fabrics, most of which would be appropriate to a living room. Busy fabrics with a repeated motif, such as paisley, are particularly good for family living rooms, as they will hide the inevitable spots and stains. Paisley is a wonderfully rich, jewel-coloured fabric, which originated in India but from the nineteenth century was produced in the Scottish town of Paisley. A couple of paisley-patterned scatter cushions and a simple pair of curtains, set into a well planned colour scheme, would offer a practical room for all seasons.

Living Rooms/*Pictorial*

When you plan your living room, you should always have an idea as to
how you would like the finished scheme to look. But it is often difficult to
know what effect individual patterns will have on the atmosphere of that
room. One sure way of injecting a definite theme into a room is with the
use of pictorial pattern. Pictorial patterns have been produced for
centuries, featuring representation of the world around the designers of
the time. So if you want your living room to be transformed into a French
château, or you fancy relaxing in an oriental haven, this type of pattern is
ideal for you.

When using pictorial fabrics and wallcoverings in a room, it's a good idea for the unseasoned decorator to purchase a large length of the material or paper to try first. A small swatch of fabric would not demonstrate the impact the pattern will have on the space to be decorated. Don't be frightened of the design. A pattern that appears large in a pattern book will inevitably look much smaller on the wall.

Pictorial designs can be used in a number of ways. You can be bold and decorate the room totally in the one pictorial design. This is ideal if you have chosen something like a monochrome toile de Jouy design, for example. In a living room, this approach would be best teamed with a neutral sofa and floorcovering, bringing the design on to the furniture via some large patterned cushions.

The walls of the formal living room shown here (left) have been decorated using a pictorial wallpaper which was very popular throughout the eighteenth and early nineteenth centuries. Based on oriental scenes, depicting ladies playing musical instruments and couples taking tea, this type of design is known as chinoiserie. A pictorial pattern like this can often be a good starting point from which to plan your colour scheme. Look at the pattern, identify the colours within that design, and use them in the same proportions in the room. Gold and blue are seen in almost equal quantities within the whole living room, as they are in the wallpaper featured as well. Also, a smaller quantity of rich burgundy appears in the wallpaper which is then used to complete the room scheme.

Alternatively, you can use the pictorial pattern in a more reserved manner, isolating its use to either a piece of upholstered furniture, the window treatment or a tablecloth, for example. However, the piece must be large enough to cope with the scale of the design.

In a living room decorated with a fussy pictorial design, simple flooring will make the best backdrop. Choose a colour from the wallpaper or fabric design for a roll of plain carpeting, opt for plain timber floors or, if you have developed more confidence in your colour and pattern combining, pick out a rug to complement the colours of the pictorial design.

Left: USING A PERIOD-STYLE PICTORIAL PATTERN IN A LIVING ROOM CAN REALLY CAPTURE THE ATMOSPHERE OF A GIVEN ERA. THIS CHINOISERIE PAPER WAS FASHIONABLE IN THE EIGHTEENTH TO MID-NINETEENTH CENTURIES. IT DEPICTS SCENES INSPIRED BY ORIENTAL TRAVEL, AND CAPTURES THE PROSPERITY AND FORMALITY ASSOCIATED WITH THAT PERIOD.

Right: PICTORIAL MOTIFS CAN ALSO BE USED IN A MODERN ENVIRONMENT. FASHIONABLE BLENDS OF COLOURS COMBINE GEOMETRIC, FLORAL AND PICTORIAL MOTIFS IN THIS REFRESHING SITTING ROOM. AND WHILE IT IS OBVIOUSLY A MODERN ROOM, THE PICTORIAL ELEMENT IN THE CURTAINS ADDS A TRADITIONAL TOUCH TO THE FINISHED SCHEME.

Living Rooms/*Texture*

Sophisticated decorating does not have to rely on complex mixing of patterns or colours, and the elaborate use of trimmings and materials. Some of the most elegant and certainly most relaxing living rooms I have come across are made up of a sensual mix of textures.

The living room is somewhere to relax and escape the rigours of a busy life – a room where you can sit back and listen to your favourite music or view your favourite film. To truly relax, I feel you should be surrounded by a soothing and tactile range of materials and not stimulated by an array of busy patterns and garish colours. If you consider texture as you plan your living room scheme, you will find the final effect, and even the design process, far more satisfying and rewarding.

Many contemporary interiors use texture as the mainstay of the scheme. Neutral schemes, for example, rely heavily on woven fabrics, timber, rattan and metal to add interest and relief to the mainly beige, cream or white colour schemes.

Texture should not be confined to completely plain rooms, however. It can be used as an integral part of a colour scheme that features patterned elements. The texture of different fabrics, stone, timber or even roughly finished walls, supplies depth and relief to a room, adding a further dimension to a well planned scheme. This can mean the difference between a successful and a magnificent room.

Textured fabrics are available in an extremely wide range of colours and designs. From the simplest hessian to the most exquisite dévoré velvet, they all add interest to a room, without the aid of a complex mix of multicoloured patterns.

Some textural fabrics, like self-patterned weaves, are used regularly for living room upholstery. Most weaves are extremely hardwearing and offer a practical and versatile option for a family sofa. The subtle quality of the pattern allows it to work with a wide range of additional patterns, whether they be brightly coloured and complex, or simple stripes and checks. This means a plain but textured sofa can be easily dressed with a range of multicoloured or textured cushions. This is a simple way of tying a piece of furniture into an overall colour scheme.

Living room flooring can be as soft and luxurious or as solid and hardwearing as you think your home can support. Your choice of texture will make a significant difference to the room's feel, however. Carpets have a warm and cosy effect on a scheme, while timber, stone, and natural flooring like coir, sisal and apple matting provide unique textural qualities and a more practical atmosphere for a family room.

Left: THE MOST TRADITIONAL OF ROOMS CAN BENEFIT FROM A LITTLE TEXTURAL RELIEF. HERE A WONDERFUL RANGE OF TEXTURES SURROUNDS THE ORNATE LOUIS-STYLE STONE FIREPLACE. THE TILED HEARTH, THE ROUGHLY FINISHED CHIMNEY BREAST AND THE METAL FIREPLACE, EACH COMPLEMENT THE OTHER BEAUTIFULLY, WHILE OFFERING THE PERFECT CONTRAST TO THE SIMPLE COTTON-COVERED CHAIRS.

Left: CREAMS, WHITE AND
NEUTRAL TONES HAVE BEEN
VERY POPULAR IN RECENT
YEARS. THEY DO, HOWEVER,
RUN THE DANGER OF BEING
FLAT AND LIFELESS. THIS IS
WHY TEXTURE SHOULD BE
HIGH ON THE AGENDA WHEN
CREATING THIS TYPE OF
COLOUR SCHEME. AS YOU CAN
SEE, THE SHINY METAL LAMP
AND THE SMOOTH BLACK AND
WHITE OF THE FIREPLACE
PROVIDE THE PERFECT
CONTRAST TO TEXTURED
FABRICS AND THE BEAUTY OF
NATURAL WOOD AND STONE.

Living Rooms/*Plain Colour*

Considering so many people are frightened of mixing patterns in their colour schemes, it is interesting to observe how many people also steer well away from using blocks of individual colour to decorate a room. Most people stick to one multicoloured pattern, teamed with a range of single-coloured items within a room. This is, in the main, a foolproof approach, as the patterned product, be it the walls or the curtains, can be used as a starting point giving a direction from which to choose the additional colours in the room. So where do you begin when decorating with plain blocks of colour?

If you have a piece of furniture or some other item you must include in the room, that will need to be the starting point for your colour scheme. Now you must decide which colours to combine with it. Consider the function of the room first. Will the room be just for adult relaxation and need to provide a soothing and calming atmosphere, or will it be busy and practical? You should also list any problems the room may have, such as a small amount of natural light, high ceilings, or limited space. All these factors will help you determine the best colours for that environment. Return to Part One and look at The Basic Principles of Using Colour (page 10) to help you pick a complementary or contrasting colour scheme for your living room.

The modern room shown here (left) has made full use of colour to create a stimulating and serviceable colour scheme for the changing needs of a growing family. Acid yellow, lime green and aquamarine (the basic colours used here) are harmonious colours, as they lie next to each other on the colour wheel and are almost guaranteed to work well together, but they benefit from the addition of an accent colour – in this case blocks of red. Red is found on the opposite side of the colour wheel and is therefore a powerful accent to the yellow and aquamarine. Use accents with caution; if you use too much of an accent colour in a room it loses its power and becomes an integral part of the scheme. Small blocks, as seen here, are the best option.

Left: A LIVELY COLOUR SCHEME IS IDEAL FOR A LIVING ROOM FOR A COUPLE EXPANDING INTO A FAMILY. A BRIGHT BLEND OF COLOURS OFFERS A STIMULATING ENVIRONMENT THAT BENEFITS FROM THE ORDERED APPEARANCE THAT BLOCKS OF PLAIN COLOUR ADD TO A ROOM. COMPARED WITH PATTERNED INTERIORS, THIS WOULD NOT LOOK CLUTTERED AND OVERPOWERING WHEN FILLED WITH THE PARAPHERNALIA ASSOCIATED WITH A BUSY FAMILY.

Right: TRADITIONAL SURROUNDINGS CAN ALSO BENEFIT FROM COLOUR-ONLY ROOM SCHEMES. HERE THE SOLID BLOCKS OF PASTEL COLOUR ADD A SOOTHING AND SOPHISTICATED ATMOSPHERE TO AN INHERENTLY TRADITIONAL ROOM AND FURNITURE.

Colour-only living rooms have a very contemporary effect and the plain blocks of individual colour give a room a very ordered atmosphere. If you want to create a more relaxed colour-only scheme, chose either calming soft blues and greens, or neutral colours. Beige, cream, off white and soft caramel all combine to create a very soothing and calm room. These subtle shades can be lifted by the addition of a contrast colour like pistachio green, soft sorbet orange or pale bluebell.

KITCHEN AND DINING ROOM *style*

Good planning is the key to successful kitchen design. A clever layout will make the difference between a kitchen that is just nicely decorated and a kitchen that is not only full of style, but also functional, comfortable and user-friendly.

The planning process should begin by listing the main functions of the finished room, in order of priority, to help you make the best use of space. Is the kitchen going to be used purely for the preparation and storage of food? Do you need to include a dining area and if so, is it just for family use? Will the room need to include laundry facilities? Will the space also be used as a home office, or for the children to do their homework?

The kitchen is undoubtedly one of the most expensive rooms in the home to design and install. Try to choose fittings that will not date too quickly, to act as a neutral framework around which various styles of furnishings can be added – and then changed at a later date.

Next you can address the question of style. Certain decorative styles are more appropriate to family homes, while others suit the bachelor pad or a young couple's flat. A country-style kitchen, for instance, may give a welcoming air to your home, but will delicate handpainted kitchen units withstand the wear and tear associated with a growing family? If you have young children, you may be better off looking at a modern kitchen with easy-to-clean, hardwearing surfaces and excellent storage facilities.

Once the function and style have been determined, you can proceed with the planning of the room. You will need to decide whether to plan the room yourself or leave the layout to an expert kitchen designer. If you do attempt this yourself, make sure you have good reference material to enable you to plan everything on paper to scale as mistakes can be costly to rectify.

Left: THIS PRACTICAL AND WELCOMING KITCHEN BENEFITS FROM SPACE, SO IT CAN INCORPORATE INFORMAL AND MORE FORMAL EATING AREAS.

Kitchens and Dining Rooms/*Geometric*

The kitchen was for many years a space in which to prepare and store food only. This, and the limited range of practical surfaces available, led to the home kitchen of the past being a very sparse and utilitarian environment. Today, however, there is a limitless range of floorcoverings, ceramic tiles, vinyl wallcoverings, worktop products and furnishing materials that can all be used very successfully in a kitchen setting. This means today's kitchen can be as comfortable and decorative as any living room, as formal as any dining room, and as practical as any utility room – which is fortunate in an age when space within the home is at a premium, and many homes have multifunctional kitchen/dining rooms.

Stripes and checks have been universally used in a kitchen setting for many years – we are all familiar with gingham curtains and tablecloths. More recently, however, home decorators have been using a broader spectrum of geometric pattern within this setting. As we spend an increasing amount of our time in the kitchen, we become more aware of the need to create a flexible environment. This means designing a colour scheme that will take the room easily from day-to-day living through to more formal entertaining. Geometric patterning is ideal for this. It can deliver a wide range of patterns and colours in a very detailed but controlled manner, creating a comfortable yet ordered, and therefore slightly formal, atmosphere.

This kitchen/dining room (left) has just such a scheme. The chosen pattern mix combines various geometric designs in a unified colour range which is fresh and welcoming. A harmonious blend like yellow, green and blue is easy to live with, and creates an uplifting atmosphere. Many design houses produce wallcoverings and fabrics similar to this range. It is a derivative of the coordinated schemes so popular in the Eighties, which matched wallpapers, fabrics and borders. The Nineties version is less obviously coordinated and, although a link between colour and motif still exists, it is more subtle. The lack of a wallpaper border here helps it look modern and less 'out of one pattern book'.

Left: THERE ARE TWO TYPES OF GEOMETRIC PATTERN: PURE GEOMETRIC DESIGNS, SUCH AS CHECKS AND STRIPES, AND MORE LOOSELY BASED GEOMETRIC PATTERNS, LIKE TRELLIS AND LATTICE WORK ENRICHED WITH SCROLLS AND FLORAL MOTIFS. THE PATTERNS USED IN THIS STYLISH ROOM HAVE A UNIFYING FLORAL MOTIF WORKED INTO THE GEOMETRIC DESIGN.

Right: STRONG GEOMETRIC PATTERNS CAN DISGUISE THE SHAPE OF AN ITEM. HERE THE PATTERN APPLIED TO THE KITCHEN UNITS CREATES AN ORDERED BACKGROUND FOR THE FLORAL DINING CHAIRS, MAKING THE DINING TABLE THE CENTRAL FEATURE OF THE ROOM.

When a kitchen layout dictates that the dining table must be central to the room, it can be difficult to avoid it being overpowered by the surrounding kitchen fittings. A clever use of surface decoration on the units can be the answer, and trompe l'oeil decoration is one option. This style of handpainting deceives the eye, creating a false impression of space and perspective. For example, geometric decoration to create the effect of sandstone block work could be used to blend kitchen units into the surrounding wall space in a stylish kitchen. Or you could apply a simple geometric pattern over the entire surface of the kitchen, again tying the design into the surrounding wall decoration, as has been achieved in this checked kitchen below. With this approach, attention is then taken away from the form of the kitchen units and the kitchen is transformed into a patterned background against which you can place a table and chairs.

Kitchens and Dining Rooms/*Floral*

Floral motifs have been popular for centuries, and because of the distinctive way floral pattern has evolved over the years, it has become widely used to reproduce period styles in many homes. As we enter a new century, the designer's approach to the use of floral pattern is once again evolving.

Below: CONTEMPORARY FURNITURE WORKS BEAUTIFULLY WITH THIS TRADITIONAL FLORAL FABRIC AND WALLPAPER. THERE IS NOW A STRONG LEANING TOWARDS THE COMBINING OF OLD AND NEW IN INTERIORS WHICH LEADS TO THE CREATION OF STYLISH ROOMS LIKE THIS REFRESHING DINING ROOM.

Traditional pattern is still very popular but, in addition to traditional styling, florals are being used in a more understated, contemporary fashion. When you use a wide range of one product, colour or pattern in a room scheme, that item will of course have a great effect on the appearance of the finished room, but in its overuse, that individual product can also lose impact. Today's leading designers have embraced this knowledge and are creating floral room schemes that are a refreshing change from the very chintzy interiors that have been popular for so long. The result is a scheme where the uncomplicated use of floral pattern is easy on the eye, allowing the design to stand strong.

The dining area featured here (near right) has been decorated using florals in exactly this way. Separate blocks of the same pattern are used to decorate this and the adjoining kitchen so that the eye is cleverly drawn from the wallpapered kitchen through to the window of the fresh contemporary dining room. In this room, a wallpaper border is used to decorate plain painted walls to give continuity of design while adding contrast to the patterned walls of the kitchen. This is a very uncomplicated approach to decorating a space, and is easy to achieve. The most important thing to consider is the positioning of the blocks of pattern and the effect they will have on the appearance of the room (see Part One, Using Floral Pattern, page 50). Contrast is also important. Many people might have matched the walls to the background colour of the curtains. This would have resulted in a softer scheme, lacking the crisp freshness that is so appealing in this room.

There is a floral pattern available to enhance every style of kitchen or dining room. Traditional or modern, pretty country cottage or even penthouse chic – all can

benefit from a version of this versatile pattern. Each floral design has its own character. One pattern may be fresh and lively with a combination of full-blown flowers in contemporary bright yellow, pinks and green; another, soft and mellow, combining stylized flowers in a softly distressed pattern, the addition of which would give time-worn elegance to a dining room or kitchen. Florals are particularly useful in a combined kitchen and dining room, as they can look fresh by day but soft and romantic for dining at night.

Below: FLORAL PATTERNS NEED NOT OVERPOWER A ROOM. THE USE OF SOFTLY DISTRESSED DESIGNS LIKE THIS ADDS A MELLOW NOSTALGIA TO A COLOUR SCHEME.

Kitchens and Dining Rooms/*Motif*

The variety of ways you apply a motif to a colour scheme is almost limitless. You can introduce them via wallpaper, fabric, stencils or stamps. Even then, they can be engraved, etched, painted freehand, appliquéed or embroidered. Whatever the medium used, they are a great decorative tool.

In a kitchen, motifs are ideal to use to decorate cupboard doors, add pattern to ceramic tiles, create a border on a coir or sisal rug or simply add detail to the leading edge of a roman blind. So if you're looking for inspiration for decorating the kitchen or dining room this may be your answer.

The variety of motifs available is as broad as the ways in which they can be applied. Traditional designs like the fleur de lys, the classical urn and heraldic motifs can all be used to add grandeur to a dining room, and work wonderfully well in a richly coloured setting when applied in gold. Burgundy, dark green, blue and terracotta are especially good background colours for this type of scheme. The same gold motifs take on a classical air when used in a neutral cream and caramel environment. This look can also be achieved with the use of other similar designs like the Greek key or classical scroll motif – ideal for a relaxing, yet elegant and stylish, dining room.

The family kitchen can be given a stimulating and humorous touch by decorating it with what I call 'whimsical' motifs. Animals, birds, vegetables, stars and other celestial motifs are all great fun when used in a family setting, but could be used in any stylized decorative kitchen scheme.

If you want to create a modern fresh look, consider using a geometrically styled motif, such as lozenges, polka dots and non-representational designs like the repeat motif featured in this kitchen (near right). These designs all add pattern to a room without confining it to a particular style or theme. There have been plenty of wallcoverings featuring this type of motif produced in recent years, but many have been used in very fashionable colour combinations unique to the time the paper was first produced and have dated quickly. Here, however, the motif has been printed in a mid-blue on a crisp white base – ageless colours, which should give this scheme longevity.

If you want to repeat the use of the same motif throughout your kitchen scheme, remember the rules for pattern-mixing given in Part One, page 43. For example, if your walls are decorated with one size of repeated motif to create an even patterned background, try using the motif in a different scale on the kitchen units or curtains, or use it purely as a border decoration. In addition, if the same motif is to be used on a central feature like a tablecloth, the design could be combined with a different patterned background, such as stripes, to make it look less 'matched'. Or the motif could be made into an overall pattern with various sizes of motif covering the fabric. Bordering such items as tablecloths with a contrasting plain or semi-plain fabric also helps to define the items within the colour scheme. If the pattern is repeated around the kitchen without any sort of framing or definition, it will merge into one and have less impact.

Left: WHITE AND BLUE IS A VERY TRADITIONAL COLOUR COMBINATION AND YET ONE THAT IS STILL FRESH. HERE IT HAS BEEN USED SUCCESSFULLY WITH A CONTEMPORARY MOTIF-PATTERNED WALLPAPER. THIS DESIGN ADDS DETAIL TO THE ROOM, WHILE RETAINING A CRISP AND CLEAN MODERN ATMOSPHERE.

Above: WHILE COORDINATION, IN DECORATIVE TERMS, IS VERY MUCH A STYLE ASSOCIATED WITH THE EIGHTIES, THE MORE SIMPLE CONTINUATION OF A THEME OR MOTIF IN A DOMESTIC ENVIRONMENT IS STILL VERY POPULAR AND IN MANY CASES CREATES A VERY SUCCESSFUL SCHEME. THIS COUNTRY KITCHEN IS FRESH AND INVITING. THE MAIN COLOUR SCHEME CONSISTS OF WHITE AND THE NATURAL TONES OF TIMBER AND STONE, WHILE YELLOW IN THE FORM OF A REPEAT FRUIT MOTIF ADDS VIBRANCY TO AN OTHERWISE NEUTRAL SCHEME.

Kitchens and Dining Rooms/*Pictorial*

Pictorial patterns are the perfect way of introducing a theme into a kitchen. The effect can be as subtle or as strong as you like. Either way, it will help to make what has always been a utilitarian space a more decorative environment.

Fabrics and furnishings are a good starting point for a pictorial scheme. Designs featuring blue and white china are a pleasant and natural choice for use in a kitchen or dining room, but many other types of pictorial patterning would work equally well. Consider fruit and vegetables of all shapes and sizes to add colour and pattern to a stylish kitchen. Window treatments should be as practical as possible, such as a simple roman blind that is unlikely to be affected by the odd inevitable splash of water in a working kitchen. It is also an ideal way of displaying pictorial patterning as the blind is seen flat, revealing much of the detailing that is, unfortunately, lost in gathered curtains. The wallcoverings too should be chosen not only for their decorative qualities, but because they also offer a washable and moisture-resistant surface.

If you would prefer to keep your fabrics or walls simple, or are looking for other places to introduce design, there are plenty of options in the kitchen. A heavily glazed ceramic tile frieze could bring detail to an open area behind the cooking range, for example. This type of tile has the benefit of supplying a practical,

Right: THE BLUE AND WHITE CHINA PATTERN ON THE WINDOW TREATMENT IN THIS KITCHEN HAS SUPPLIED ADDITIONAL COLOUR AND PATTERN TO A TRADITIONAL ROOM. IT HAS ALSO INSPIRED THE USE OF A PICTORIAL STENCIL MOTIF ON THE WALLS, CONTINUING THE BLUE AND WHITE CHINA THEME. THIS IS THEN ENHANCED BY THE COLLECTION OF REAL BLUE AND WHITE CHINA. IT IS ALSO EASY TO SEE HOW, JUST BY CHANGING THE PICTORIAL PATTERN USED, YOU COULD GIVE THE AREA A NEW LOOK WITHOUT CHANGING THE MAIN AND MOST EXPENSIVE ELEMENTS WITHIN THE ROOM.

easy-to-clean surface in addition to its decorative impact. Tablecloths are another way of introducing pictorial detail to a room. Quite often the kitchen table is in the centre of the room, so any patterning on its surface is brought into the heart of the scheme. You can also edge tablecloths with a contrasting plain or patterned border. Checks are an ideal option. They will not only add more detail and draw the eye to the pictorial pattern in the main cloth, but can then be used

for coordinating table napkins, or in an upholstery fabric for the dining chairs. It is this type of detail that will make all the difference in your finished room.

Below: PAINTED KITCHENS HAVE BEEN ENJOYING A REVIVAL IN RECENT YEARS. THE DECORATOR OF THIS COUNTRY KITCHEN HAS CHOSEN TO STENCIL PICTORIAL PATTERNING ON TO THE SURFACE OF THE KITCHEN UNITS — A BRAVE AND EFFECTIVE WAY TO USE PATTERN IN THE SPACE AVAILABLE.

Kitchens and Dining Rooms/*Texture*

Interior design is far more than matching wallpapers and curtains. A scheme should stimulate the senses, having an effect not only on the space being decorated, but also on the mood of the people living in it. Textural interiors seem to do this extremely well and I have a particular love of them. Texture adds a further dimension to a scheme, making you want to touch, as much as look at, your surroundings.

Many of the products used to introduce texture into a scheme look very much at home in a kitchen environment. Timber, stone and metal all have unique qualities that make them practical and aesthetically pleasing finishes to use in this setting. Texture can also work within different styles of kitchen and dining room, traditional or modern. The contemporary dining room featured on the far right has a very soothing atmosphere. The bleached, natural tones of the timber flooring, softly grained storage units and curvaceous chairs are very calming and mellow. However, placed against a pure white background they gain strength, adding character to the room. Textural contrast is supplied via the cream woven rug and the simple wooden blind. It is not the wood of the blind that supplies the interest, as timber is already featured heavily in the room, but the textural pattern produced by the repeating wooden slats.

You can easily add texture to your kitchen by giving your walls an interesting paint finish such as rag rolling, dragging or colourwashing. Paint finishes have once again become very popular in recent years, and many of these decorative effects are ideal for use in a practical environment, like the kitchen/dining room, as they offer a washable surface.

The flooring is another element of the room that offers the opportunity to create a textural contrast with the units or walls. You have to be sure that the flooring you are using in a kitchen scheme is as practical and, in most instances, as hardwearing as possible, so consider natural flooring, such as stone. Stone floors are both easy to maintain (they may require sealing once every 12 months) and hardwearing, but in addition they add texture to a room. Glazed ceramic tiles are also very easy to clean, and offer an excellent hardwearing surface, but even those produced to emulate natural stone

do not have the textural beauty of the real thing. And, in my experience, natural stone is warmer underfoot than any glazed product.

In any room where texture is going to be used, it is important to have some form of smooth finish. Just as a well planned colour scheme needs tonal relief, a textural scheme also needs variation. Smooth linen fabrics provide a refreshing contrast to a naturally textured product like slate or coir matting, for example. In the same way, shiny hard granite works perfectly with the more mellow texture of wood.

Left: THE GOLDEN TONE OF THESE COLOURWASHED WALLS IS ECHOED BY THE INSERT FEATURED IN THE WONDERFUL NATURAL STONE FLOOR. TEXTURE CAN BE ADDED TO A SCHEME IN MANY DIFFERENT WAYS, AND A NATURAL PRODUCT LIKE SLATE ALSO BRINGS DETAIL TO THE FLOOR.

Above: SIMPLE LINES, CALMING NEUTRAL COLOURS AND PLENTY OF TEXTURAL VARIATION ARE THE KEY TO A SOOTHING CONTEMPORARY INTERIOR.

Kitchens and Dining Rooms/*Plain Colour*

Many people find busily decorated kitchens and dining areas hard to live in. When you consider the kitchen is often the first room you enter in the morning, or the first you see when returning from a busy day at work, you can instantly appreciate the benefits of a room decorated in simple, plain, uncomplicated colours.

Colour is the most powerful aid to the home decorator. It can capture the atmosphere of distant places or eras, and can dramatically alter the aesthetic appearance of a space. Regardless of how simple and functional the decor of a kitchen is, there is no excuse for the room lacking character – and colour can make all the difference.

There are a number of things to remember if you are going to decorate your kitchen or dining room with a colour-only scheme. In the main, cool colours recede to make a space appear larger, and slightly more formal, while warm colours will advance to make a room look smaller, more cosy and welcoming. The tonal variation of the colour you choose is also important. The deeper the tone of colour, the less reflective it becomes and the closer it appears to be. Therefore, a dark green room will look smaller than the same room decorated in a light tone of the same colour (see Part One, page 14).

By using this knowledge, you can make your kitchen appear to be what it is not. A galley kitchen, for example, would benefit from the clever use of colour to minimize the 'corridor' appearance. A warm, advancing colour could be used on the short walls of the room, with either cool colours, or a distinctively lighter tone of the same colour, on the remaining longer walls. This will act to draw the shorter walls together, visually pushing back the long walls and making the room appear shorter and wider.

Colour and tone can be used in the same way to make a tall dining room ceiling look lower, and feel more cosy at night. By using a darker tone of colour on the ceiling, or, if the ceiling is extremely high, also on the frieze, you can make the walls appear shorter. The same effect is achieved with warm advancing colour on the ceiling and cool receding colour on the walls.

The kitchen here (near right) incorporates simple lines and blocks of one colour used in different tones to produce a simple yet distinctive look. Single-colour schemes are the perfect backdrop for the plethora of crockery and cooking utensils found in all kitchens. It has become common for these items, once confined to a closed cupboard, now to be seen and to act as an integral part of the overall colour scheme, illustrating how the current trend in design is to embrace a more casual living style.

Left: Green is a very balanced colour. Here it creates a focused and calming environment – ideal for a productive kitchen. Green is also a good background for earthy colours like terracotta, brown and the natural tones of wood.

Above: This dining room is very peaceful, and shows how a simple combination of blue and cream, with no superfluous pattern, can produce a traditional Scandinavian elegance.

BEDROOM
style

The bedroom can be the one room in the home that is truly reflective of the occupant's personality. It should be a space in which you can completely relax and forget the stresses of everyday life – an environment designed just for you.

As with all well designed rooms, time and consideration should be given to the layout of the bedroom to ensure that there is ample storage space and perhaps a sitting area, a working space, a new dressing room or even en-suite facilities for the bedroom. If you are planning the layout yourself, try out many different schemes before you decide. It is always easier to spot a bit of wasted space on paper than in the actual room with large pieces of furniture in the way. Having a layout to scale on paper will also show you things that you might not have thought of. For instance, you may find that you can fit in that bedside table that you really want, if you reduce the dimensions of it, or maybe even just the width, by a small amount. In many cases you will find that additional space can be freed up within the room, just by rethinking the positioning of the bed, for example.

Once you have decided on your layout, you can turn your attention to your choice of colour and pattern – and truly indulge yourself with the fabrics that make you feel most pampered, sensual and relaxed.

Left: THIS BEDROOM RELIES ON ITS HARMONIOUS COLOUR SCHEME FOR ITS RESTFUL AND RELAXING ATMOSPHERE. SIMPLE FLOORING AND FURNITURE COMBINE WITH THE COLOUR SCHEME TO PLACE THE FOCUS ON THE COSY-LOOKING BED.

Bedrooms/*Geometric*

Geometric patterns, such as stripes, checks, lattices and trellises, all have a place in the bedroom. They are ideal for decorating a space that requires a particularly masculine air, or for a spare bedroom, which needs to appeal to all ages and to both genders. Some designs, for instance checks, can help you create different styles, such as fresh country, baronial Scottish (when used as a tartan) or, when used in soft slate blues and greens, Scandinavian.

There are now many inexpensive ranges of striped and checked fabrics available which can be used to great effect as wall upholstery, allowing you to invest in an indulgence without being too extravagant. Fabric wallcoverings add a soft luxury to a bedroom scheme, especially when applied over a padded base, and the finished effect should more than justify its extra cost.

Most fabric designs can be used for upholstering walls, and many geometric designs have additional qualities that can be used to address the commonly encountered problems when decorating a bedroom. Stripes, for example, are easy to pattern-match and have the benefit of giving height to a low-ceilinged room, or area within a room. A four-poster bed draped with vertical stripes will also add visual height to a bedroom, while curtains made up in a striped fabric will give extra length to a small window.

Traditional tartan designs are available in most decorative products. Carpet, fabric, wallcoverings and ready-made bedding are all produced in this distinctive geometric design, which can be used to great effect in a strong masculine bedroom. Mix tartans with checks and stripes in uniform colours of varying scale to produce a very comfortable and traditional bedroom scheme. They work best against a block of traditional colour; single-coloured striped wallpapers or softly distressed walls are two excellent options.

Geometric pattern can also be introduced to the floor area of a bedroom. Patterned carpets are one obvious solution, and single-coloured trellis designs can provide a good base for many colour schemes. There are a small number of striped carpet designs available which will add something a little different to a room. They also give you the opportunity to add apparent length or width to a room, depending on the direction in which the carpet is laid. Timber flooring can also be used in this way as the line of the boards helps create a similar optical illusion. Also consider painting floorboards with a geometric pattern, such as squares, to give a smart clean look. Remember to bear in mind the scale of pattern you use, so that it is in keeping with the size of the bedroom.

Right: CHECKED FABRICS OFFER THE PERFECT COMPANION TO A WIDE RANGE OF PATTERNS. IN THIS SCANDINAVIAN-STYLE BEDROOM, THEY SIT PERFECTLY WITH THE WOVEN LATTICE BEDSPREAD, WHICH FEATURES AN EMBROIDERED FLORAL MOTIF. THE SAME MOTIF IS PICKED OUT IN THE UPHOLSTERY FABRIC.

Right: SIMPLE STRIPES CAN BE USED TO CREATE A VERY DISTINCTIVE AND ELEGANT SCHEME, INCREASING THE IMPRESSION OF HEIGHT IN A BEDROOM. HERE BLUE AND CREAM STRIPES ARE USED TO UPHOLSTER THE WALLS AND ARE COMBINED WITH A MID-BLUE FABRIC TO CREATE THE SMART SOFT FURNISHINGS. A CONTROLLED USE OF LIGHTING ADDS INTEREST TO THE FINISHED ROOM.

Bedrooms/*Floral*

The bedroom is the first room you see each morning when you wake, and the last you see before falling to sleep at night, which is why many find floral patterning the perfect base for a scheme. Flowers can be bright and uplifting for a fresh start to each day, yet are natural and easy on the eye when you want to relax. Floral designs can also provide a romantic edge to a scheme, creating the ideal room in which to love or be loved.

Floral pattern can be used in various ways within the bedroom. A scheme based entirely on floral designs, with the careful layering of differing scales of pattern, will create either a country cottage or country house style of interior, depending on the style of the dominant pattern. Small rosebuds and blowsy cabbage roses will add a cottagey charm to a room, while the more refined, chintzy floral designs, featuring mixed flowers such as tulips and peonies, will add country house style to a traditional room.

As with all designs, the colour of the pattern also plays a very important role. Floral designs in various shades of blue through to blue-green have a very cool and relaxing quality. Warm peaches, pinks and terracotta patterns, however, are more welcoming and cosy – the ideal answer for warming up a bedroom that gets little or no sun.

Floral pattern can also be used to address problems within a colour scheme. A relatively small room might be overpowered by a striking floral pattern on the walls. However, if it is decorated with plain ivory curtains and simple colourwashed walls, pattern can then be introduced on to the bed area, defining the bed within the room while allowing the surrounding area to appear as large as possible, due to its simple decoration.

Floral pattern can be used to decorate all types of surface within the bedroom. Wallpapers of numerous designs and colours are available in anything from the

Right: SOFT, RAG-ROLLED WALLS FORM THE BACKGROUND FOR THIS WARM-LOOKING BEDROOM AND ARE THE IDEAL BASE FOR THE FLORAL CURTAINS WHICH DOMINATE THE ROOM.

Far right: REMEMBER FLORAL PATTERN NEED NOT BE TRADITIONAL, IF YOU USE IT SIMPLY. HERE A COOL BLUE FLORAL MOTIF HAS BEEN USED MAINLY AROUND THE WINDOWS AND ALSO TO HIGHLIGHT THE BED. TEAMED WITH NEUTRAL COLOURS EVERYWHERE ELSE, THE RESULT IS A SOOTHING YET FRESH AND THOROUGHLY MODERN BEDROOM.

most delicate silk to the most practical solid vinyl. (In the bedroom there is going to be little wear and tear on the walls, so you can allow yourself the indulgence of opting for your preferred pattern and material, for once, rather than putting practical considerations first.) Stencils and stamps can supply additional floral patterning to painted surfaces, such as headboards, dressing or bedside tables – or the walls themselves. Softly distressed or colourwashed walls can look very effective with the addition of an aged stencil motif. Floorboards and natural floorcoverings also take on a new lease of

life when bordered with floral designs, applied in the same way, for a traditional look.

For a more contemporary feel to the design, floral motifs can be applied in a bold and expressive manner. Large appliquéed flowers can look wonderful on a quilted bedcover, while simple voiles or muslin can be transformed by the application of large artificial blooms in a repeated pattern. A more subtle approach would be to sew little pockets into the sheer fabric, and insert small, delicate artificial flowers. The finished effect is almost magical, with diffused floral blocks of colour.

Bedrooms/*Motif*

In the opening paragraphs of this section, I suggested that a bedroom was a very personal environment. This doesn't necessarily mean you have to create a scheme that is significantly different to those you have created throughout the rest of the home. If you have already used a particular style that you feel comfortable and relaxed with, then why not continue it through to the bedroom too? The choice is yours.

The traditional decor used in the living room, for example, can be continued to the bedroom with motif patterns such as the fleur de lys. This particular motif originated in France and has been one of the most popular motifs throughout history, although it was particularly prominent in Renaissance, Gothic revival and Medieval interiors. The bedroom featured here (main picture) uses the fleur de lys motif in a repeat pattern to decorate the surface of this wonderful regal four-poster. The woven pattern is reversible, allowing the designer to use the fabric in many versatile ways. The back drape to the bed is covered totally by the fleur de lys design in gold on a burgundy background. Its reverse side then provides a versatile border design to the sumptuous velvet cushions that adorn the top of the bed. This sort of approach is cost effective and also shows the ingenuity of the designer when using one simple fabric design. Velvet and gold braid have been used together with the main fleur de lys motif and a regal gold and burgundy stripe to dress this bed, which is the main feature of this masculine bedroom.

Although the room is spacious, a bed like this cannot help but dominate it, so the surrounding decor has been kept as simple as possible. No extra pattern has been introduced, other than the velvet and fleur de lys used again to highlight the chair and link it back to the bed.

Of course, traditional styles are not the only form of motif available to the home decorator (see Part One, page 54). There is now a wide range of modern and contemporary styles that can be used effectively in the bedroom. Many of these tend to be figurative and are loosely based on geometric patterns, and have evolved into the softer, stylized motifs that are being used by contemporary design houses. With this modern style the designer's approach is slightly different from that for traditional interiors. Now the motif is generally used as an overall pattern rather than as a border or individual embellishment and the pattern is used to draw the eye to a specific area of a room, turning it into a feature.

Left: BURGUNDY AND GOLD
WITH A HISTORICAL MOTIF IS
A PERFECT COMBINATION FOR
A TRADITIONAL DECORATIVE
SCHEME. HERE SUMPTUOUS
FABRICS AND THE CLEVER USE
OF PATTERN FOCUSES
ATTENTION ON THE GRAND
FOUR-POSTER BED THAT IS
THE CENTRAL FEATURE OF
THIS ROOM.

The fresh blue and white contemporary bedroom seen here (right), with a modern motif design, is the perfect example of this contemporary styling. The patterned blue wallpaper has been used as a panel behind the bed to draw attention to the area, making it the focal point of the room, without the bed itself having to be too busy. The simple metal lines and fresh uncluttered linen give the bed a stylish and inviting air.

Above: PANELS OR BLOCKS OF MOTIF PATTERN CAN BE USED
WITHIN A ROOM TO ATTRACT ATTENTION TO A PARTICULAR AREA
OR ITEM; FOR INSTANCE, THIS CONTEMPORARY BEDROOM HAS
USED THIS DESIGN APPROACH TO MAKE A FOCAL POINT OF THE
BED. IT IS INTERESTING TO SEE THE USE OF PATTERN WITHIN A
ROOM THAT MANAGES TO RETAIN A CRISP, CLEAN ATMOSPHERE.

Bedrooms/*Pictorial*

The bedroom is the one room in the house where we can expect a certain amount of privacy – a room that is normally only seen by close friends and family. Therefore it does not have to follow the main theme of the rest of the house, and you can allow yourself to create a distinctive personal look that might not have worked elsewhere. Pictorial pattern is ideal for making a powerful statement. If you work in a very bland yet busy environment all day, pictorial pattern could help you to create a wonderfully exotic bedroom in which to relax at night.

Pictorial detail can be delivered to a room via the obvious route of fabric and wallcoverings, or by the more individual form of handpainted mural work. Think of the impact a handpainted scene might have on your finished bedroom. The room could be transported as far as your imagination will take you. Imagine your bed positioned within a crumbling Greek temple, surrounded by classical architectural detailing. Or you may prefer your room to look out across sculpted English gardens and on to a distant wooded landscape. Whatever your ideal haven, murals and trompe l'oeil can take you, and your bedroom, there – and there are plenty of interior designers and artists happy to provide the service.

If your preference is the introduction of pattern in manageable blocks within a traditional colour scheme (on the curtains, bedspread or upholstery, for example), there are a number of designs that will work wonderfully in an imaginative setting. Take a look at oriental designs. They first appeared on European textiles during the mid-seventeenth century, inspired by the expansion of trade in the orient and the importation of Chinese artefacts. They were popular up to the late nineteenth century, but still look striking today.

If you fancy creating a more classical look, fabrics and wallpapers depicting cherubs or ancient buildings are the ideal base, especially when they are combined with colours like soothing cream, vivid yellow and black and white.

Another design with a historical tradition is toile de Jouy. One of the most popular pictorial patterns currently used, it originated in France in 1770 and depicts scenes of oriental life, important events in history and

Right: IF YOU HAVE AN ARTISTIC FLAIR OR IN FACT KNOW SOMEONE WHO HAS THE ABILITY TO DECORATE WITH SURFACE PATTERN, WHY NOT CONSIDER USING PICTORIAL REPRESENTATIONS, DRAWN FREEHAND, TO DECORATE YOUR ROOMS? THIS VERY STYLIZED FLORAL PICTORIAL DESIGN HAS BEEN USED ON THE WALLS IN TRADITIONAL TONES OF BLUE AND GREY, AND SITS WELL WITH THE HEAVILY CARVED FURNITURE.

Above: THIS BEDROOM HAS PLENTY OF CHARACTER. THE BLEND OF ORIENTAL PICTORIAL PATTERN AND THE COLLECTION OF SHIP PAINTINGS CREATE A ROOM WITH A WELL TRAVELLED NOSTALGIC AIR, WITHOUT ALLOWING THE PICTORIAL FABRICS TO DOMINATE.

views of rural life. It was very popular in Europe and America well into the nineteenth century, and is now used to add a traditional quality to a room. The delicate and detailed pattern, traditionally in a single colour on a white or ivory base, mixes extremely well with checks and stripes of various scales and colours. A bedroom with its walls and soft furnishings depicting a single toile design, with simple neutral and crisp white bedding, has a traditionally soothing quality.

If you are the sort of person who likes to take a more light-hearted approach to life, whimsical designs featuring fictional characters can offer a bedroom a little humorous relief. There are a number of ranges of this style of pictorial pattern available from the leading interior design houses.

Bedrooms/*Texture*

Textural interiors work on a number of levels, providing the decorated room with both visual and tactile interest by creating a space that is pleasing to the eye and stimulating to the touch. The bedroom is the ideal area for concentrating on this type of decorative scheme, as it will help to create a soothing and sensuous environment.

There is a wide range of fabrics and soft furnishings currently available with different textural patterns, thanks to the growing trend in neutral schemes and our increasing confidence in pattern-mixing. This gives you the opportunity to mix and match the light and the heavy, the coarsely woven and the smooth, to wonderful effect.

Sheer voiles with delicate woven motifs, for example, are now commonplace. Their fine delicate texture can add softness to a simple window blind, or can make a central feature of a bed when draped from a gilt corona or half-tester above the bedhead. This light-weight type of fabric can be combined successfully with other textural woven products of a heavier weight. Monochromatic woven stripes and herringbone weaves are all robust designs which are perfect for use as upholstery in a bedroom setting, especially in delicate creams and neutral tones, and which will all benefit from the contrasting softness of a fine voile or muslin.

We are all familiar with the patchwork-patterned quilted bedspread found in pretty cottage-style bedrooms, but in the textural bedroom a wonderful fabric known as matelasse, derived from the French word for mattress, makes the perfect bedcover. This double layered fabric, normally in ivory or white cotton, gets its distinct patterning from the puckering caused by the threads which join the two fabrics together into one thick cloth.

Leather and fur fabrics are also seeing a growth in popularity now. The production of excellent faux furs and man-made leathers has allowed the designs to once again be widely used where they have been shunned for so long. As this look becomes more popular, inevitably the natural product is also having a bit of a revival, but

Above: ALL NEUTRAL COLOUR SCHEMES NEED TONAL VARIATION TO BE VISUALLY INTERESTING. HERE THE TONAL SPECTRUM VARIES FROM BLACK THROUGH TO BROWN, CREAM AND WHITE. THE FUR THROW ADDS A TOUCH OF SOFTNESS TO AN OTHERWISE QUITE AUSTERE ROOM.

fortunately, no longer in any great volume. Furs have always been valued for their warmth and, in centuries past, beds were made up of layers of fur fabrics. Today, these are seeing a return to the bedroom, as fur throws become an enviable accessory for the well dressed bed. Fur, cashmere, satin and crisp linen all have their own

individual textural qualities. However, they make a wonderfully indulgent combination, ideal for dressing a bed in the most luxurious of textural bedrooms.

The soothing and relaxing bedroom here (right) gains its textural quality from the combination of carved wood, and woven and printed textiles. There is a variety of patterns in the scheme, but because they are all of one colour, the emphasis is on the texture instead. Simple white walls and a black floor make the perfect canvas for a textured scheme as these non-colours (black and white) do not compete with the delicate detail of the fabrics and their textures.

Above: ACCESSORIES CAN BE USED TO INTRODUCE EXTRA TEXTURE TO A ROOM, ENSURING THAT IT IS AS STIMULATING TO THE TOUCH AS IT IS TO THE EYE. HERE A COLLECTION OF CARVED, NATURAL, PAINTED AND DISTRESSED WOODEN ARTEFACTS ADDS BOTH VISUAL INTEREST, DETAIL AND COLOUR TO THIS SIMPLE WHITE AND CHOCOLATE-COLOURED BEDROOM.

Bedrooms/*Plain Colour*

We know colour can affect your mood and alter the visual proportions of a room, so it is important not to underestimate its power, especially when you are decorating a bedroom and want to create a certain type of atmosphere. Some families of colour work together to produce a certain effect, while other colours combine to produce a completely different interior.

Harmonious colours are those that lie next to each other on the colour wheel (see Part One, pages 12 and 68). Pinks and violets, for example, yellows and oranges, or blues and greens will combine to produce harmonious schemes. These colour combinations lack sharp contrast and are therefore easy on the eye, and ideal for decorating a bedroom.

The cool-coloured harmonious scheme is the most relaxing of all. Blues and greens are very calming cool colours. Paler blues in particular will also make a space appear larger, making it the perfect choice for a small bedroom – although if it is a chilly room it might need the addition of a small amount of yellow to warm the scheme up a bit.

Most two-colour schemes can benefit from the introduction of a small amount of a third colour. This will act as an accent colour, and add visual interest to the scheme. In a harmonious colour combination the additional colour can be chosen from colours adjacent to the two main ones, as they are seen on the colour wheel. A blue and green scheme, for example, would benefit from a small amount of either yellow or violet, while yellow and orange would be enhanced by a touch of green or red.

Neutral colour combinations are another good choice for the bedroom. A room decorated with various tones of white, cream, beige and brown through to black is very natural-looking. It relies heavily on tonal variation and texture to be successful, but when planned correctly it can create a very sensuous and sophisticated bedroom scheme.

If you are a lover of colour, but shy away from mixing colours and patterns, the monochromatic bedroom scheme may be the perfect solution. A monochromatic room is based on just one colour, but various tones and shades of that colour are combined in the scheme, to create an interesting, subtle interior. The joy of this type of scheme is that you can, if you wish, base your choice of colour entirely on the effect it will have on your mood. If you like to escape to your bedroom in the evening to read a book, for example, a green scheme may be perfect. Green is a very focused and balanced colour, the ideal environment for reading or study. A blue colour scheme will relax and calm (in fact, this colour is known to lower your heart rate, so I cannot think of better surroundings in which to relax). Pinks and reds, however, are more stimulating and add warmth and a little passion to a room.

Left: A HARMONIOUS SCHEME OF BLUES AND GREENS IS A RESTFUL CHOICE FOR A BEDROOM. BLUE HAS THE REPUTATION OF BEING A COLD COLOUR, AND IN MANY CASES THIS IS TRUE. HERE, HOWEVER, A WARMER LAVENDER BLUE IS COMBINED WITH THE WARMTH OF NATURAL GOLDEN TIMBER TO CREATE A WELCOMING AND RELAXING BEDROOM.

Far left: THE BEDROOM IS A VERY PRIVATE PLACE, SO THE DECORATION SHOULD REFLECT THE OCCUPANT'S PERSONAL STYLE. THIS SUMPTUOUS INTERIOR HAS A VERY OPULENT AIR, WHICH HAS BEEN CREATED BY THE USE OF GENEROUS AMOUNTS OF QUILTED VELVET IN BLOCKS OF DRAMATIC COLOUR.

CHILDREN'S ROOM
style

The main difference between a child's room and one for an adult is that the child's room should be able to change and develop as years pass. It is fair to say that a baby's bedroom is more a reflection of the parent's needs and decorative preferences than the baby's. So approaching the decoration of a nursery is a matter of creating a safe and warm environment with ample storage. It is not until the child has grown a little that consideration has to be given to the child's decorative preferences. This is when the design challenge begins.

Every little boy and girl will be influenced by a number of trends during childhood. Various cartoon or fictional characters will become the 'must have' of that particular season and the shops will undoubtedly be full of soft furnishings and bedding depicting your little one's new hero. But although it may be tempting to dress a room from floor to ceiling in this favourite theme, you can guarantee that what your child delights in today will be out of favour tomorrow. Unless you are happy to redecorate every couple of years, it is best to keep to a decorative scheme that will not date. This does not mean you should steer away from these fashion items totally; just use them as accessories within a more lasting scheme.

Designing a child's room in such a way that it can grow with the child is not as difficult as it may sound. If you combine curtains and bedding, wallcoverings and flooring in fun patterns and stimulating colours that are ageless, it will be the perfect backdrop for changeable accessories, pictures and toys that reflect both the child's personal preferences and age.

Left: A CHILD'S BEDROOM CAN GIVE YOU THE OPPORTUNITY TO CREATE A WONDERFUL AND IMAGINATIVE DECORATIVE SCHEME. IF YOU DO OPT FOR A FULL-SCALE MURAL, TRY TO AVOID IMAGES ASSOCIATED WITH A CURRENT FAD, AND CREATE A MORE GENERAL FANTASY WORLD LIKE THIS ONE.

Children's Rooms/*Geometric*

When you approach the decorating of a child's bedroom, it is always wise to remember that children will naturally introduce additional colour, pattern and texture in the form of their toys, games and books to a room. It is therefore true to say that, regardless of the type of pattern and colour you choose, the room will nearly always be unmistakably that of a child.

Above: GEOMETRIC WALLCOVERINGS ARE PERFECT FOR A CHILD'S CHANGING BEDROOM, AND EACH SEASON WALLPAPER DESIGNERS PRODUCE THIS TYPE OF PRODUCT IN THE COLOURS OF THAT PERIOD. THIS ROOM DEMONSTRATES THAT IT IS THE IDEAL BACKDROP FROM WHICH TO DRAW ADDITIONAL COLOUR INSPIRATION FOR SOFT FURNISHINGS AND ACCESSORIES. HERE THE CREAM BACKGROUND ENSURES THAT THE ROOM IS NOT OVERPOWERED BY ITS PATTERN.

Geometric patterns, in the form of checks, stripes, tartans and trellises, are perfect for creating a colour scheme that will grow with a child. This type of pattern can be used in a number of ways. Geometric wallpaper, for example, can create a decorative backdrop to additional geometrically styled or plain blocks of colour within a room. The bedroom featured here (left) uses a very open two-colour checked pattern as a background to plain soft furnishings in the same colour as the lines of the pattern on the walls. While the curtaining and bedding is produced from plain textiles, the designer has used a combination of both colours to add detail to the various items in the room. The curtaining, for example, has a simple triple pleat heading, but has an insert border on both leading and hem edges to define the curtaining while adding decorative detail. The bed, too, benefits from this approach, but in addition to the plain colours, a small red checked fabric has been introduced to line the bedcover. This red gingham fabric is also used in the personalized lettering of a small scatter cushion, adding a touch of individuality to the finished room.

The colour of the geometric pattern you choose can completely alter the room's mood and effect. Checks and tartans in soft pastels will produce a very delicate interior, ideal for a young child, while bolder checks in shades of traditional bottle green and red add a more sophisticated, masculine and established air to a room. Simple gingham designs in reds, blues and slate green bring a Swedish simplicity to a child's bedroom, especially when combined with sheer curtaining at the window for a soft and romantic finish. Whatever sort of scheme you finally settle on, you can combine it with further geometric patterns on the various soft furnishings or upholstery and you can be sure of a successful design for your child's room.

Once you have settled on your wallcoverings and curtaining, you can turn your attention to the floor, which in a child's bedroom needs to be as practical and washable as possible. Geometric pattern makes an ideal choice for carpeting, as it looks smart and will disguise the inevitable spot or stain. Even more practical are the patterned vinyls now available, which make a serviceable and decorative floor finish for a child's bedroom or play area. Vinyl floorcoverings allow you to introduce geometric patterns like a tartan, for example, in a variety of deep colours.

Below: GEOMETRIC DESIGNS, LIKE THE TRADITIONAL GREEN AND RED PATTERN FEATURED ON THE BEDCOVER HERE, CREATE AN AGELESS ENVIRONMENT IN WHICH A CHILD CAN GROW. USING SUCH PATTERN IN BLOCKS WITHIN A PLAIN DECORATIVE SCHEME ENSURES THE ROOM RETAINS AN UNCLUTTERED AND SPACIOUS ATMOSPHERE.

Children's Rooms/*Floral*

Floral patterns remain the preferred choice of many when decorating the bedroom, regardless of the fact that most adult bedrooms are shared by both men and women. In a child's bedroom, however, floral pattern is going to be more popular with the girls than with the boys! That said, once mixed with other patterns, such as geometrics, florals lose their overt femininity, and can be used to create a room that is suitable for both genders, ideal for when brothers and sisters share the same room.

If, however, you are sure you are not going to be decorating for a tomboy, and want to produce a room which is feminine and delicate, floral designs are ideal. Pick a scale and colour of floral pattern to suit the size and character of the bedroom. Florals with soft, cool-coloured backgrounds, for example, may be a good starting point for a bedroom that has limited space, as this colour scheme can create a very airy and expansive environment. A room which doesn't get much sun, however, would benefit from warmer colours, such as peach and pink, for example, which are found on one side of the colour wheel and produce cosy and welcoming interiors. Yellow is also an excellent colour choice for a bedroom. It creates an optimistic and sunny atmosphere, bound to lift the spirits of troubled teenagers, even on the dullest of days – and it is perfect for a nursery if you do not know whether you are decorating for a girl or a boy.

A cottage-style bedroom can take on a nostalgic charm when decorated with country flowers in delicate pastel shades. The bedroom featured here (near right) benefits from floral pattern used not only for soft furnishings, but also as a soft background in the form of a repeat floral motif wallpaper. The wallcovering features a pale, single-colour motif, which coordinates beautifully with the flowing floral stripe used in profusion in this scheme. If, however, the wallcovering had been of a deeper tonal value, or included an additional colour,

Right: PINK AND BLUE IS A TRIED AND TESTED COMBINATION WHEN DECORATING A CHILD'S BEDROOM. WHILE THIS ROOM HAS BEEN DECORATED WITH CHILDREN IN MIND, THE PATTERNS USED HAVE ENSURED THAT THE ROOM WILL PROVIDE A SUITABLE ENVIRONMENT IN WHICH THEY CAN GROW.

the room would have appeared to be smaller. With an eye to the small proportions of the room, blue is the ideal colour for the flooring. Not only does it offer a practical colour for this finish, but it is also a receding colour, which ensures the floor area appears as large as possible.

Floral designs should not be limited to traditionally styled children's bedrooms. There is a wide range of contemporary-style floral fabrics available that can be used to create a stylish and modern interior for our fashion conscious youngsters. Bold and colourful, daisies, tulips and sunflowers all offer floral solutions that are far removed from a pretty rosebud cottage style.

Below: WALLS AND FLOORS DECORATED IN VARIOUS TONES OF A SINGLE COLOUR CAN BE USED TO ADDRESS SPECIFIC PROBLEMS IN A ROOM. SHADES OF BLUE, FOR EXAMPLE, WILL MAKE A SPACE SEEM AS RESTFUL, YET EXPANSIVE, AS POSSIBLE. HERE A YELLOW FLORAL PATTERN HAS BEEN USED, WITH GREAT EFFECT, TO WARM UP A BLUE ROOM. IT ALSO OFFERS THE PERFECT PARTNER FOR THE PRETTY BLUE BEDCOVERING.

Children's Rooms/*Motif*

There is a wide range of motifs available to create the right atmosphere for your child's bedroom, but try to think beyond the obvious collections of teddy bears, toy soldiers and bunny rabbits. They are undoubtedly perfect for a younger child's room, but will date and become inappropriate as the child grows older. If you can't resist splashing out on a few of the more babyish motifs, restrict yourself to using them in a controlled manner. Some scatter cushions, a lampshade and possibly a blind for the window are inexpensive items that could be replaced by more sophisticated motifs when the time is right.

Stencilling and stamped motifs are a simple and inexpensive way of introducing pattern to a child's room. You could use them to revamp old furniture to make it suitable for the nursery, or create a very personalized design for your child. Motif patterns that will grow with your child can also create stimulating and pretty interiors. Heart shapes are one perfect example. They can be used in either a traditional or a contemporary setting, and when combined with pink and blue ginghams and checks they can create a very attractive folk-art style of interior.

The bedroom featured left combines a heart motif wallcovering with checks of various proportions. The blue heart motif is on a yellow background, firmly establishing the colour scheme, which the furniture and floor fit into. The bedcover and upholstery fabrics are made up of a small geometric pattern, one incorporating the blues and yellows, the other introducing an additional accent colour to the room in the form of green detail on a blue and white background. Many colour schemes made up from an almost equal amount of two colours will always benefit from the introduction of a small amount of a third accent colour. This form of styling always creates a very relaxed but effective look.

Another popular motif for children's rooms is the flower. Pretty, delicate rosebuds will obviously impart a country-style atmosphere to a room, but more stylized designs can be used to great effect in a playful and contemporary style of bedroom. The room featured right uses just this type of daisy motif to create a fun and stimulating environment. The toys and cot ensure you are in no doubt that the room is designed for a baby, but exchange this item of furniture for a day bed, for example, and it would create the perfect setting for a growing teenager too. The designer of this room has approached the decorating with humour and enthusiasm. Her confident use of colour has hugely benefited the scheme, and details like the motif spilling on to the ceiling area, and the choice of old denim jeans for upholstery, add a unique twist to the room.

Left: A STIMULATING ENVIRONMENT IS AN IDEAL SETTING FOR A BABY'S BEDROOM. THIS ROOM NOT ONLY FEATURES DETAILING THAT WILL APPEAL TO ADULTS, LIKE THE CHOICE OF UPHOLSTERY FABRIC, BUT ALSO GIVES A GROWING CHILD A GREAT DEAL OF COLOUR AND PATTERN TO FOCUS ON.

Far left: THE HEART MOTIF FEATURED IN THIS PRETTY BEDROOM WAS POSSIBLY THE INSPIRATION FOR THE ADDITIONAL USE OF PATTERN WITHIN THE ROOM. THE HEART CONTAINS A SIMPLE CHECK WHICH IS COMPLEMENTED BY THE USE OF GEOMETRIC FABRICS ON BOTH THE CHAIR AND THE BED.

Children's Rooms/*Pictorial*

Right: This room demonstrates how a basic scheme will allow for the introduction of new pictorial pattern as the child grows. The colours are also practical. Below the dado, a rich red paint offers the room both colour and an easy-to-maintain surface within an environment susceptible to sticky fingers and the occasional artistic outburst. The colour chosen for above the dado is light and expansive, giving the room an air of spaciousness while retaining its warm atmosphere.

Pictorial designs are often considered when designing for a child. Who hasn't been tempted to opt for scenes of teddy bears' picnics and brightly coloured train stations for a toddler's room? The options on theme are endless, however, and never mind how strong-willed your little one is, you are bound to find something that pleases you both. It is always wise to avoid decorating a room in products that all feature the same pictorial theme. The clever positioning of a specific pattern within a room means that these items can be changed without having to completely redecorate when the child has outgrown or tired of that particular theme.

The cheerful bedroom featured here (top) has been decorated with a range of fabrics and colours, all unified by the rocking horse pictorial design. The main use of the pattern is limited to the wallpaper border, the duvet covers and the window blind. These are the perfect places to display pictorial pattern as they provide flat surfaces on which to fully appreciate the design. As a window treatment, a blind is the preferred way to use pictorial pattern, as a great deal of detail can be lost when the fabric is gathered to create other types of treatments. The main window has been dressed using plain cream curtaining finished with a pretty striped valance. If the child outgrew the pictorial motifs used in this setting, it would take little time or expense to update the room, as the neutral curtaining and general colour scheme could be retained to work with a variety of new patterns.

The epitome of pictorial decorating in the child's bedroom is undoubtedly the use of mural and trompe l'oeil. The phrase trompe l'oeil simply means 'trick of the eye', and this handpainted form of decorating adds a perspective and depth to a painted scene on the walls. The lucky inhabitant of the fairy-tale bedroom shown here (bottom) has the pleasure of waking each morning in a fantasy environment. The furniture used has been designed from a child's perspective. It is rather 'cartoon-like' in its styling, as the base of each item is narrower than the top. This gives each piece of furniture the illusion of a grander scale, and the overall effect is that of a magical environment in which to grow up.

Handpainted scenes like this can create any environment. This form of decoration is only limited by your imagination. Your child could grow up in a room depicting fairground or circus scenes. Alternatively, they could go to sleep looking out on a luscious country landscape with air balloons floating peacefully in the distance. Remember, though, that if you are splashing out on an expensive mural you will be reluctant to decorate over it in a couple of years' time, so do try to stick to a theme with a lasting quality.

Right: MURALS AND TROMPE L'OEIL ARE THE PERFECT WAY OF INTRODUCING A FANTASY QUALITY TO A CHILD'S BEDROOM, ALBEIT A RATHER PRICEY ONE IF YOU ARE LACKING IN THE NECESSARY ARTISTIC TALENT YOURSELF. HERE THE MAGICAL QUALITY OF THE ROOM IS ENHANCED BY THE FAIRY-TALE STYLE OF FURNITURE.

Children's Rooms/*Texture*

A younger child requires a safe and warm environment, but quite often the remainder of the decorative choices are tailored to the parents' preferences as opposed to those of the child. Decorating a room for an older child has a completely different brief from that for a baby or toddler.

Teenagers or older children have specific needs that must be taken into account. Study is an important element of their growing life and takes up a great deal of time and concentration. Creating an environment that is conducive to this is very important as children need an area or space in which they can focus on their work. At this point in their lives, then, you may decide that too many patterns and bright colours can be distracting, and a more neutral, textured interior may be the perfect solution. If you do opt for this simple approach to decorating, accept from the start that a child's room will never be a minimalist showpiece. Children are great hoarders and the room will soon become covered with their treasures. Perhaps think instead in terms of giving them a starting point of interesting contrasts and textures, on which they will stamp their own personality.

Look at all the different elements of the bedroom when introducing textures. Sheer voiles embellished with woven detail and a motif will add texture and detail to a window dressing. Walls can be colour-washed, dragged or given some other subtle paint effect for a practical finish. Additional woven patterning can be introduced to floors and upholstery with a careful selection of material. Timber flooring and furniture, too, can bring character to a textural scheme. Whether natural or distressed, it can bring mellow or aged detail that will stand up to the hardest of knocks.

Another good reason for removing the emphasis from soft furnishings is the recent increase in childhood illnesses, such as asthma. It has now become a regular part of an interior designer's brief to create rooms that are suitable for a child with such a condition and certain textural environments are perfect for this. The most important thing to ensure is that the surfaces are easy to clean and no havens for dust are produced, such as pelmets, picture rails, and swags and tails.

The bedroom featured here (left) has a mellow textural quality due to the style of timber used throughout, which provides practically the only pattern and colour in the room. The matt black areas of wall act as a contrast to the timber, ensuring that its inherent pattern becomes apparent. The only other colour is introduced via a simple duvet cover. When coupled with anti-allergy bedding, this type of interior creates the perfect bedroom for a child with asthma, but offers an ageless interior suitable for any growing child. Toys can be kept neatly away in specially designed storage spaces, ensuring that the surfaces are kept uncluttered and dust free.

Left: TIMBER CAN ADD A WONDERFULLY MELLOW TEXTURE TO A COLOUR SCHEME. HERE THE PRIMARILY WOODEN INTERIOR OFFERS A STYLISH SOLUTION FOR A GROWING CHILD AND COMPENSATES FOR THE LACK OF SOFT FURNISHINGS IN THE ROOM.

Above: SIMPLE YET EFFECTIVE, IN TERMS OF STYLE AS WELL AS PRACTICALITY, THIS BEDROOM OFFERS A FOCUSED ENVIRONMENT IN WHICH A CHILD CAN STUDY. THE BED DESIGN SUPPLIES TWO SLEEPING AREAS WITH AN INTEGRAL DESK AT WHICH TO DO HOMEWORK OR READ. THE TIMBER USED IN ITS CONSTRUCTION HAS BEEN LIGHTLY STAINED AND SANDED TO GIVE IT A SOFT TEXTURAL QUALITY, IDEAL FOR ITS SETTING AGAINST ROUGHLY PAINTED BRICKWORK.

Children's Rooms/*Plain Colour*

Most parents despair at the amount of toys and accessories that are found strewn across many a child's bedroom. Regardless of the amount of storage space available within the room, there never seems to be enough. So is there an easy way of making these toys look an integral part of a colour scheme, as opposed to a messy addition?

One way of achieving this is by creating a colour-only environment. This type of colour scheme does not include any traditional patterns, and while it can create a very stimulating and colourful interior, it can often benefit from the addition of pattern introduced by accessories such as toys. Pattern does not have to be achieved via the traditional forms featured in this book. Pattern can be created yourself by careful positioning of blocks of colour or accessories within a room. While we may not consider a small square of colour to be a pattern, when it is repeated at regular intervals around a room, it does create the effect of traditional patterning. Equally, what is the difference between a pictorial border featuring representations of toys, and a shelf positioned around the room displaying the real thing? You are in control of the environment and can create some stunning effects with just a pot or two of paint.

Another way of making a child's room appear as simple as possible is the defining of space within the room. If the bedroom you are decorating is large enough, you could divide it into playing and sleeping areas and define those areas by using different blocks of colour. All toys and playtime accessories can then be limited to the playroom part of the room where they can sit happily against a colour-only background, appearing as uncluttered as possible. The other advantage to dividing up a large room is that when the child has outgrown the 'play' area, that space can either provide an en-suite facility or be used to produce a studio environment in which a teenager can feel safe yet self-sufficient.

In the bedroom featured here (near right), the space has been divided by the use of a partition wall, featuring windows of various shapes and sizes through which children (and adults!) can peer into the adjoining area. Consider how you might use your decorative scheme to

help in the education of your young ones. You could use large painted letters and numbers to create blocks of colour on the walls, floors and storage units. Alternatively, you could include a textural element, by having large letters covered in fun fabrics attached to a plain wall.

Producing a simple colour-only environment, where plain colour decorates the surrounding walls and floors, is the ideal way of creating a flexible and lasting colour scheme for your child. By limiting your use of soft furnishings to patterns and colours that are ageless, it will be your child's accessories and playthings that will decorate the room, dictated by and reflecting the age of the occupant.

Left: ONCE THE TOYS AND ACCESSORIES ASSOCIATED WITH YOUR CHILD ARE REMOVED, THE COLOUR-ONLY SCHEME WILL STILL PROVIDE A PLEASANT ENVIRONMENT FOR THE TEENAGER. HERE A ROOM ONCE DIVIDED INTO A PLAY AREA AND SLEEPING QUARTERS NOW HOUSES A SIMPLY DECORATED BEDROOM WITH EN-SUITE KITCHEN.

Far left: BY INCORPORATING VARIOUS COLOURS AND SHAPES INTO A PARTITION WALL IT IS POSSIBLE TO PRODUCE A STIMULATING, EDUCATIONAL ENVIRONMENT FOR YOUR CHILD TO ENJOY.

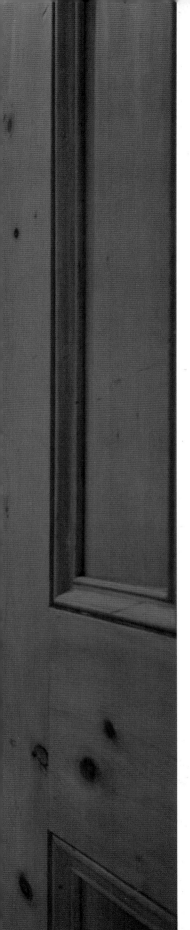

BATHROOM
style

Your bathroom can be far more than a purely practical space. Bathroom design and decoration has never been more exciting or varied, giving you the opportunity to create the pamper parlour of your dreams. Whether you want a room to refresh and invigorate you, or one in which to ease away stress at the end of the day, there will be a style to fit the bill. But first you need to do some homework.

If you are lucky enough to be designing your bathroom from scratch, you need to decide upon far more than simply the colour scheme. Before you embark on the decorative planning of your bathroom, you should work out the most successful layout by experimenting on paper first.

Draw the room to scale on graph paper, ensuring you include all information, such as plumbing, radiators and architraves, on the plan. Then draw your preferred choice of fittings, such as the bath, lavatory, bidet and so on, to the same scale and cut them out as templates (the measurements are normally available in the brochures). You can then move these templates around the floor plan until you find the best layout for the room, allowing for the opening of doors and windows, and for people passing one another. One aspect that is commonly forgotten at this stage is leg room. It may be nice to squeeze in both a shower and a bidet, but what is the point if you end up with no leg room at the lavatory!

I find it best to leave finished plans for a day or two before confirming them as the best option. Reviewing your choice with a fresh eye may help you add additional features, like a raised floor (ideal for hiding pipework), or a wall to divide up the room into specific areas. All these things will have a profound effect on your finished room and give you a solid base on to which you can add colour and pattern to create your ideal environment.

Left: A BATHROOM SCHEME CAN REALLY BE ONE TO HAVE FUN WITH, ESPECIALLY IF THE ROOM WILL BE USED BY THE WHOLE FAMILY. HERE AN UNDERWATER THEME HAS BEEN CARRIED THROUGH TO THE VERY LAST DETAIL.

Bathrooms/*Geometric*

Geometric pattern is most easily introduced to the bathroom via the wallcovering or the tiling. Ceramic tiles have been a central part of bathroom design for hundreds of years because of their practicality and because of the design opportunities they offer even if left unadorned. Throughout history, however, geometric pattern has featured heavily in their decoration. As early as the fourteenth century, checks, trellises and overlapping circles were popular, and geometric black and white borders or designs constructed from single-colour square tiles have been a bathroom favourite for nearly as long.

Even today, we call repeatedly on the designs of the past when we decorate our bathrooms. The recent revival of Victorian-style interiors has made a particular impact on bathroom design, and illustrates how, even when incorporating modern features such as the power shower into this environment, we rely heavily on designs that have a sense of history. The bathroom here (left) has been greatly influenced by the traditional Victorian-style geometric-patterned flooring which has set the scene for the other fixtures and fittings. When creating a period look such as this, you are reliant on reproduction or reclaimed products, but fortunately, recent years have seen a return to the mass manufacture of such items.

For a contemporary look, mosaic tiles are currently hot news. Try using them in your bathroom to add detail in the form of a border, or even to decorate whole walls or floors. The patterning depicted in mosaics is very broad, with designers creating a wide range of patterns or pictorial representations as well as more simple geometric designs. Geometric borders in mosaic often feature the traditional Greek key border and Vitruvian scroll pattern, originally a Greek form of ornamentation. Both of these decorative styles can be used in a traditional or contemporary setting, depending on the colour of tiles that you opt for. For a contemporary look, turn to bright tropical or citrus colours such as lime greens and lemon yellows, but for a period look, try more muted shades or the classic black and white.

The recent popularity of back-to-basics styling and Shaker design has made its impact on bathrooms too. The bathroom featured here (right) is given an effective look by the combination of simple timber cladding, a natural floorcovering and a naive-looking paint technique, but the room takes on a fresh, bold air thanks to the geometric patterning on the walls. This is a very simple technique achieved by stamping blue paint over a white base coat with squares of foam, to create a soft-edged geometric-checked pattern. Blue and white is a classic colour combination which has been used within the bathroom setting for years, but can still look modern and never fails to look stylish.

Left: BLUE AND WHITE IS A TRADITIONAL COLOUR COMBINATION FOR BATHROOM SCHEMES, BUT HERE IT HAS BEEN GIVEN A MODERN LOOK THANKS TO THE GEOMETRIC PATTERNING OF THE INFORMAL PAINT TECHNIQUE ON THE WALLS. THE FLOORCOVERING OFFERS A TEXTURAL QUALITY, BUT ALSO ADDS RUSTIC WARMTH TO THE SCHEME, COMPLEMENTING THE TIMBER AND TRADITIONAL FITTINGS.

Far left: A RELATIVELY PLAIN, ALTHOUGH SPACIOUS, BATHROOM CAN AFFORD TO USE GEOMETRIC PATTERN IN A LARGE BLOCK TO INTRODUCE CHARACTER AND DETAIL TO A SCHEME. HERE TRADITIONAL FITTINGS COMBINED WITH A STRIKING CERAMIC TILE FLOOR HAVE PRODUCED AN ELEGANT PERIOD SCHEME.

Bathrooms/*Floral*

Floral pattern introduces fresh natural imagery to a bathroom and can be applied in some form on practically every element of bathroom design, from the fittings themselves to the wallpaper and window dressings. If you are considering a floral scheme and are replacing your fixtures and fittings, think about investing in a new white suite. White is a good colour for a bathroom suite; it looks crisp and fresh which suits nearly all, but especially floral, schemes. It also has the bonus of actively making cream paint or wallcoverings look richer and making other colours appear more vibrant, guaranteeing your new scheme instant success.

As in other rooms, the floral motif should be chosen to enhance the particular style or theme of your bathroom. In other words, you should choose a style of flower to suit the look you are trying to achieve – be it kitsch, cottage, romantic or contemporary. Don't feel restricted by the age of your home, as modern florals in contemporary colourways can be used to create stylish interiors in both new and more traditional properties. The window dressing in this bathroom (near right), for example, has a soft and flowing contemporary floral pattern laid over a base of hazy aquamarine, combined with a traditional bath tub and screen.

Do not feel restricted to using purely florals – mix and match by combining with geometric-style fabrics as has been done here. A small aquamarine check has been used alone on the screen, chair and bath mat, and combined with a floral motif to create the larger checked pattern of the blind and screen. Both are the perfect companions for the main floral pattern.

If your bathroom is one where children like to splash about, full-length curtains would be better avoided; consider using ceramic tiles to provide a practical wall finish from floor to ceiling. These can obviously incorporate a floral motif or design if you wish. However, by keeping this element relatively plain, you can vary the

Above: MODERN FLORAL PATTERNS CAN CREATE A FRESH AND LIVELY BATHROOM ENVIRONMENT. GONE ARE THE DAYS WHEN THE BATHROOM APPEARED COLD AND AUSTERE. WELL-BALANCED COLOUR SCHEMES INCORPORATING WARM COLOURS, SUCH AS THIS GREEN AND THE GOLDEN WOOD, HAVE NOW REPLACED THE UTILITY FEEL ORIGINALLY ASSOCIATED WITH THIS ROOM.

Above: FULLY FITTED BATHROOMS IN A COUNTRY HOUSE STYLE ARE THE PERFECT SETTING FOR FLORAL PATTERN. THE DETAILING ON THE FITTED BESPOKE FURNITURE IS ENHANCED BY THE DELICATE QUALITY OF FLORAL DESIGN.

atmosphere of the room by introducing pattern to the other walls, away from the bath or above the tiling. Many wallpapers feature floral patterns, traditional and modern, but in the bathroom you must be guided by practicality. Whatever wallpaper design you choose, it should be on a solid vinyl base, as most bathrooms experience high levels of moisture which normal paper will not be able to withstand.

Accessories must also be taken into consideration when decorating a room – even a bathroom. They can be used in one of two ways: either to enhance the atmosphere created by the decorative scheme or as a dominant feature within the room. Imagine a deep blue, monochromatic colour scheme (tones of one colour) finished with a profusion of oriental accessories. Ginger jars and large urns, featuring a typical oriental stylized floral pattern, can turn an ordinary bathroom scheme into something striking and individual. Their pattern adds detail to the room, while the white porcelain combines with white fittings to provide a stunning contrast to the blue scheme.

Bathrooms/*Motif*

Motif patterns can be incorporated into a bathroom in a wide variety of ways. Use them to add interest to the tiles, wallcoverings, fabrics, accessories or even on to the sanitary fittings themselves. Remember, though, that motifs need not act as an overall theme featured on every element within the room; they can simply act as an accessory, setting the tone of the room rather than dominating it.

Below: THIS TRADITIONAL BATHROOM HAS BEEN DECORATED WITH THE USE OF SUBTLY ELEGANT DECORATIVE PAINT TECHNIQUES. THE OVERALL SCHEME IS MONOCHROMATIC AND RELIES ON THE PAINT EFFECT FOR BOTH TONAL INTEREST AND TEXTURAL PATTERN. THE FABRIC DRAPE WITH A REPEAT FLORAL MOTIF ADDS A SOFTNESS TO THE FAUX MARBLE AND STONE DESIGN.

Right: THIS MODERN BATHROOM GAINS CHARM FROM THE DECORATIVE BLUE WALLPAPER USED ABOVE THE TILES. THIS FEATURES A SMALL SCROLL MOTIF IN A VERY MODERN STYLE, WHILE THE BORDER DISPLAYS STYLIZED FISH IN AN EXPANDED RANGE OF COLOURS. BLUE ROOMS CAN APPEAR COLD, BUT THE INTRODUCTION OF PINK AS AN ACCENT COLOUR GIVES THIS ROOM A CERTAIN WARMTH.

If you are looking for inspiration, turn first to the past. Classical motifs have been popular for many years in the bathroom setting. Greek key borders, Vitruvian scrolls and classical urns all add traditional elegance and can be incorporated as a stencilled motif on to a painted surface, or featured within a border on a wallcovering or ceramic frieze.

The seaside, nautical pursuits and sea creatures are other common sources for motif designs and are easy to introduce to a bathroom. You could attach natural sea shells to sheer curtaining for an original window dressing, or look out for sea shell curtain decorations which simply hang from the rings on the curtain pole that already suspend the curtains. This decorative approach can be teamed with driftwood-framed mirrors and accessories to produce a stylish room with a seaside air rather than a seaside theme.

Natural forms such as flowers and leaves can also be used to great effect, introducing a cottage or country house atmosphere in their natural form, or a more contemporary look when used in a stylized form and applied, with a stencil or freehand, in a metallic-finish paint effect.

In a more traditional bathroom setting, the fleur de lys design can add a rich and opulent air to a colour scheme. This motif, featured in gold and set on a base of deep red, blue or traditional green, will give a bathroom a grand historical atmosphere, even if your fittings cannot.

There is no excuse for your bathroom floor being dull these days. Vinyl floorcoverings and ceramic floor tiles feature motif designs, quite often as decoration on small inserts within a patterned tile. Stencilling and stamping a natural timber floor is also an option – although make sure it is well sealed with varnish as it can be very susceptible to water damage.

For those with the benefit of a large bathroom, motifs can be introduced on additional items of furniture not generally associated with a bathroom to create an extremely comfortable interior. In a traditional setting, comfort and style can be introduced to this room via the use of armchairs upholstered in a fabric featuring your chosen motif. Or a circular table dressed in a motif fabric can provide an elegant area on which to display the lotions and potions required for pampering.

Bathrooms/*Pictorial*

Right: THE TOILE DE JOUY FABRIC IS WELL USED WITHIN THE LIVING ROOM AND BEDROOM ENVIRONMENTS. HERE, HOWEVER, IT IS USED TO GREAT EFFECT TO CREATE A COMFORTABLE AND TRADITIONAL BATHROOM. ORIGINALLY PRODUCED IN FRANCE IN 1770, IT IS MOST COMMONLY SEEN AS A SINGLE-COLOUR PRINT IN BLUES, REDS OR GREENS AND IS EASILY SOURCED TODAY.

Pictorial representations can be used to introduce a specific style to your bathroom, be it romantic, contemporary, quirky or traditional. Find a pictorial design that appeals to you for the window dressing, wallcovering or shower curtain and use it to inspire the rest of your bathroom's decoration. The restrictions limiting the use of various designs to different rooms are slowly diminishing and the bathroom can now be as styled and as comfortably decorated as any living room or bedroom.

In busy households the bathroom may be the only area where you can find a moment's peace. It is therefore natural to yearn for a bathroom which is a haven to bathe and relax in. This is where a pictorial pattern comes into its own, creating a unique atmosphere in which to pamper yourself. I have seen some clever use of mural work in this setting, some of which has extended to the bathroom fittings themselves. Handpainted detail can link your bath and sink into the overall scheme. And even stepping into a shower cubicle can transport you to a magical world when a mural depicting a fantasy environment has been painted on the shower walls!

If a full-blown mural is rather extreme for your tastes or budget, then there are other ways of introducing effective pictorial design on a lesser scale. Plenty of ceramic tile designs feature panels decorated with scenes from nature or taken from history. Many a bathroom has been graced by a Grecian goddess pouring water from a classical urn, or a cascading waterfall.

Another very simple yet effective way of introducing pictorial pattern, and creating the impact associated with it, is with a shower curtain. Rather than buying a ready-made design from the shops, you can create something unique from a pictorial fabric that catches your eye. It merely has to be lined with clear plastic to be made into a practical shower curtain, and then it can be suspended in the normal way. Alternatively you could make up a pair of curtains to be drawn back on either side of the bath, creating a very dramatic focal point for the room.

Pictorial fabrics have an obvious home within the themed bathroom, especially those featuring a nautical or seaside theme. If no fabrics immediately win your heart, however, there are other more interesting ways of introducing some pictorial design. Recently, I found a wide range of ceramic plaques on the high street which can be used with great effect within a colour scheme or, more dramatically, against a plain painted background like the seascape featured here (right).

Above: NAUTICAL THEMES ARE AN OBVIOUS, BUT NEVERTHELESS PERENNIALLY POPULAR, CHOICE FOR THE BATHROOM. THIS FUN BATHROOM USES BRIGHT FISH WALL PLAQUES TO DECORATE A STRIKING PAINTED BACKDROP OF THE SEA BED, ILLUSTRATING HOW PICTORIAL DESIGN CAN BE THREE-DIMENSIONAL AS WELL.

Bathrooms/*Texture*

The successful textural scheme relies on pattern being introduced via textural quality rather than colour or visual decoration. In fact, many textural products are ideal for use in the bathroom. Natural materials like stone and timber are the perfect contrast to the smooth, shiny porcelain and plastic commonly seen in bathroom fittings. Metal, too, has its place in the textural bathroom: wrought iron, chrome and cool steel all have qualities that can add both tonal variation and contrast in this environment.

Right: EITHER BATHROOMS CAN BE DECORATED IN A PURELY HISTORICAL OR REGIONAL STYLE, OR THE DESIGNER CAN CHOOSE TO CREATE AN INTERIOR UNIQUE TO THEIR PERSONALITY AND TASTE. THE BATHROOM FEATURED HERE DOES NOT FALL INTO AN EASILY CATEGORIZED STYLE. HOWEVER, ITS TEXTURAL QUALITIES COMBINE TO CREATE AN INTERESTING AND UNUSUAL EFFECT.

Far right: IT IS EASY TO ASSUME THAT MATERIALS SUCH AS STONE AND WOOD CAN ONLY BE USED TO PRODUCE RATHER AUSTERE DECORATIVE SCHEMES, BUT THIS BATHROOM SHOWS HOW NATURAL MATERIALS CAN CREATE A WARM AND WELCOMING ENVIRONMENT.

The bathroom featured here (left) is a wonderful example of how natural materials are often all that are needed to create a stimulating and successful scheme. Bleached timber adds a subtle colour to the floor area while the layout of the boards and the gentle texture produced by the grain of the wood provide pattern and detail. When using timber in a natural colour scheme, it is always a good idea to introduce tonal variation by including different woods or stains. There are many differing types of timber products available, all with a unique tonal quality. Here we see a golden pine used in conjunction with oak-stained beams and the bleached timber floorcovering.

Consider every aspect of your bathroom and the opportunities for textural contrasts each offers. Even the ceiling has been given a textured plaster effect while the wall to the foot of the bath has been given a simple washed effect to create the illusion of a textured surface. The main feature of the room is the stunning stone wall.

Textured materials come naturally in a wide range of colours so it would be unfair to say that this type of scheme is only available in 'natural' and neutral colourways. Natural stone, for example, comes in a wide range of designs and colours, from subtle creams through to vivid burnt reds and violets, which can introduce bold colour into a room scheme.

Textural products appear more prominent when used against a non-colour background such as black, white or cream. The bathroom featured here (below right), for example, has simple white walls which act as the perfect backdrop for the coloured natural slate, rich floorboards and the geometric-style rug. For a more contemporary look though, try mixing texture and bright colours. Even if the bathroom is within a traditional property, with stone walls for example, a painted finish on the textured stone, vivid blocks of colour and the contrast of shiny chrome fittings will create a stunning interior.

Bathrooms/*Plain Colour*

The colour-only bathroom contains no traditional pattern. The detail and interest is
introduced only via texture or plain use of colour – perfect for those with more simple tastes.

When planning a colour-only bathroom, consider the various type of colour schemes available and their effects on a space (see Part One, page 14). Harmonious and contrasting colour schemes have varying qualities. Contrasting schemes are very vibrant and generally have a strong impact on a room. The colours used are found on opposite sides of the colour wheel and create a lively mix. Harmonizing schemes, however, are created by combining colours that are direct neighbours on the colour wheel. These are easy on the eye and tend to make relaxing room schemes.

The bathroom featured here (left) combines green and yellow, a harmonious partnership which, when you consider it, means that one is strongly related to the other. In this case, green is produced by adding blue to yellow. Here green offers a practical solution for the flooring, while yellow is used on the walls to bring sunshine and brightness to the room. The window is dressed with an unobtrusive blind and detail is limited to the pattern created by the plants and paraphernalia seen by the side of the bath. As with many harmonious schemes, this room has benefited from the introduction of a contrasting accent colour. In this case red, introduced in the towel and the plants, has been chosen to pep up the overall scheme.

You can have a great deal of fun using colour within a bathroom setting, and if you have the luxury of devoting a bathroom within your home specifically to your children, this type of scheme is ideal. For example, large blocks of a single vibrant colour used to cover the main area of walls, can act as the perfect foil for multi-coloured areas of ceramic tiles. There is now a wide range of plain tiles on the market, many of which come with border tiles in varying widths and designs that can

Left: THIS TRADITIONAL-STYLE ROOM DOES NOT
NEED ANY PATTERN TO CREATE THE RIGHT
ATMOSPHERE. HERE PLAIN BLOCKS OF COLOUR ARE
COMBINED WITH A TRADITIONAL SUITE TO PRODUCE
A SIMPLE ELEGANCE.

of the interior. The pattern, from a distance, appears relatively plain, creating the impression of a simple, stylish room. Close up, however, additional pattern is revealed between the stripes, softening the effect and making the room a more interesting environment in which to work. Green was a good choice of colour for a room leading directly to a plant-filled roof terrace beyond, but it is always a wise choice for a study. Green has a balancing effect on a room's occupant, helping them to focus on the task in hand.

In many homes there is not enough space for a separate room to be a dedicated office, and somewhere to work or study needs to be incorporated into a multifunctional room. This might be a corner of a spare bedroom, the dining room, or even the hall. Many halls are large and under-used areas of the home, which makes them ideal for providing additional functional space.

The hall here (below right) would offer the storage required from a home office, together with ample working space. The large central table could double as a practical desk, while the area beneath the table could provide a home for files and paperwork. The bookcases here serve two purposes. They offer practical storage for the reading material connected with the office or study, and with the family in general. In addition, they have been built with a false central panel – decorated with faux book spines – which conceals a storage cupboard. A controlled use of geometric pattern in the window blinds and rug link with the pattern of the bookcases and unite the traditional scheme. One interesting detail of this room is the mirrored chimney breast. Mirrors can be used to make a room appear as large as possible. In this case, the area is finished off by the addition of a traditionally framed painting.

Left: WELCOMING AND SPACIOUS, THE HALL IN THIS TRADITIONAL HOME IS THE PERFECT ENTRANCEWAY, YET ITS INITIAL APPEARANCE BELIES ITS PRACTICAL ATTRIBUTES. ONLY WHEN YOU LOOK CLOSELY CAN YOU SEE THAT THE BOOKCASE CONCEALS A HIDDEN STORAGE AREA, SO THAT HOME OFFICE EQUIPMENT CAN BE HIDDEN AT NIGHT.

Far left: STRIPES ARE A VERY VERSATILE FORM OF GEOMETRIC PATTERN, CREATING EITHER A MODERN OR A TRADITIONAL ATMOSPHERE. HERE A STRIPED GREEN WALLCOVERING IS USED TO GREAT EFFECT WITHIN A HOME OFFICE INTERIOR, COMBINING WITH DARK WOODS TO PRODUCE AN ANTIQUE LOOK IN A SERIOUS PROFESSIONAL SETTING.

Home Offices and Studies/*Floral*

When you are creating a working environment within a multifunctional room, it is important to create an atmosphere that is homely and to consider whether the work space should complement the surrounding area or make a natural transition from it.

The key is to make a division between the space in which you will work and the remainder of the room without losing the character of the overall room. Clever use of pattern and a well planned layout can help you achieve that. The addition of a simple, decorated screen, for example, might be all that is needed to conceal a computer and desk from general view. Alternatively, a division created by the introduction of a false wall within the room is often a good solution. This can sometimes help to give better proportions to a living room that is long and narrow, thereby creating a space in which to work comfortably, while making the room more aesthetically pleasing.

In the smart study shown here (near right), a part wall divide makes a clear distinction between the work area and the rest of the room, while the continuity of colour scheme helps to prevent the room from looking too divided. By extending the carpet and paint colour into the smaller part of the room, and using the same dressing at the window, neither part of the room loses its character or its feeling of spaciousness. Notice also how the floral curtains provide the work area with the same sense of traditional grandeur as the rest of the room. Without them, ·that space would lack the comfortable air that the other part offers.

Floral pattern is a perfect choice for a working area set within a cosy living room or guest bedroom. I think it is fair to say that most people find they can concentrate and work best within an environment that is quite clean and ordered, so an overly fussy floral scheme should be avoided. Instead use flowers to enhance the period or regional style required for that particular room and combine that pattern with a more simple, ordered, non-floral design such as stripes, a lattice, or a simple repeat pattern.

The office or study area shown here (far right) has been decorated in such a way that it would fit easily

Above: IF THE ROOM YOU HAVE ALLOCATED AS YOUR STUDY LACKS SPACE AND APPEARS A LITTLE CLAUSTROPHOBIC, CONSIDER HOW YOU MIGHT INCORPORATE THE SPACE INTO AN ADJOINING ROOM BY REMOVING THE DIVIDING WALL.

into a surrounding bedroom or living room. It also demonstrates how florals can be used to soften a scheme for this sort of area without making it too busy, fussy, or overtly feminine. Notice how the contemporary floral design has been combined with stripes and an open lattice design on the chair to create a look that is inviting and cheerful, but not too distracting.

Above: THE COLOUR AND PATTERN YOU CHOOSE TO USE IN YOUR WORK SPACE WILL HAVE A STRONG EFFECT ON YOUR MOOD WHEN WORKING IN THAT ENVIRONMENT. WORKING AT HOME REQUIRES A LOT OF MOTIVATION, BUT STYLIZED FLOWERS USED IN VIBRANT AND UPLIFTING COLOURS WILL ENSURE YOU REMAIN STIMULATED AND RARING TO GO.

Home Offices and Studies/*Motif*

Motifs can give a study or office some character, but you need to be careful that the motif you choose suits the mood you would like to create in what is essentially a place for work. A motif that is too large, colourful or otherwise distracting will look out of place, and may give the wrong impression to visiting business acquaintances.

On the other hand, do not be deterred from using motifs in your scheme. This style of pattern introduces detail and can be used to integrate a work area with the remainder of a multipurpose room. Motifs such as the fleur de lys, the Greek key border and heraldic designs introduce a sense of order and dignity to a home office, while looking just as successful within a living room, dining room or bedroom.

If your home office is situated within a modern property, why not give your chosen motif a fashionable twist to make the room fresh and appealing, and to ensure it is in keeping with the contemporary furnishings throughout the rest of the home. Even traditional motifs, such as hand-stencilled scrolls, look exciting given a metallic hue, and their fluid lines will add a softness to a room without allowing it to be too feminine or overly fussy. Also take a look at Celtic motifs, which are gaining in popularity all the time. These are formal and abstract enough to suit an office and will work in both modern and antique settings, whether they are used as a single motif or incorporated into a pattern featuring borders of the same style.

Right: IN A MULTIFUNCTIONAL ROOM IT IS WISE EITHER TO USE STORAGE WHICH CAN COMPLETELY CONCEAL THE WORKINGS OF YOUR HOME OFFICE, OR TO USE FURNITURE THAT WILL TIE IN WITH THE OTHER PIECES WITHIN THE ROOM. HERE PINE FURNITURE COMPLEMENTS THE FLORAL MOTIF ON THE WALLCOVERING AND THE CURTAINS. A FLORAL MOTIF MAY SEEM INAPPROPRIATE FOR A WORK SPACE, BUT IT CAN LINK THIS AREA TO THE REST OF A MULTIFUNCTIONAL ROOM. THIS PARTICULAR DESIGN IS SOFT ENOUGH TO CREATE A RELAXED AIR, BUT NOT OVERLY DELICATE SO IT IS STILL AN EFFICIENT ENVIRONMENT.

Above: REPEAT MOTIFS MAY NOT BE THE FIRST CHOICE FOR A SERIOUS HOME OFFICE SETTING. HOWEVER, USED APPROPRIATELY, THEY CAN EFFECTIVELY INTEGRATE A WORKING AREA INTO AN ACCEPTABLE DOMESTIC SETTING, AS THIS MUTED WALLPAPER SHOWS.

If you are planning to start a new company, why not consider choosing a motif for your company logo that can then be incorporated into the decor of your office? A Celtic motif may be the perfect solution if you are running a business that is allied to the craft industry, for example, or a simple crossed knife and fork would make an interesting and slightly humorous motif for a catering company run from home.

In the home office the size of the motif you choose is particularly important, especially as so many offices tend to be one of the smallest rooms in the home. Busy floral motifs used in excess will make the space appear smaller, so limit their use to a frieze or to highlight specific pieces of furniture or furnishings within a room. Remember that a motif always has more impact if its use is limited. So, if you do choose to use a motif pattern as a logo for your company, one prominent display will provide a stronger image than the same design repeated excessively throughout the room.

Home Offices and Studies/*Pictorial*

If your home office is situated in one of the smallest rooms in the home, consider a scheme that will make the area appear as large as possible. Decorating the walls in light colours or colours from the cool side of the colour wheel will help, but clever storage design and the general decor will have the greatest impact.

If you require a large amount of storage within your home office, why not consider building simple cupboards along one wall? These could then be decorated with a handpainted mural, for example, depicting the view to an adjacent room or imaginary window. This could give the illusion of space, or even the extra view you dream of. Perhaps a view of your favourite holiday spot will relax you when the going gets tough or inspire you to be more creative when you have writer's block. Or maybe an imaginary scene appropriate to your line of business or a hobby would be more suitable. When deciding where to site a mural, bear in mind the scale of your room, and remember that creating the illusion of further space at the end of a long narrow room will have the effect of making the room appear even longer and, therefore, narrower.

Pictorial design can also be incorporated into your working space via soft furnishings and wallcoverings. However, I would be cautious as to the style or image you settle on, as, unless the pictorial imagery is being used as a tool to improve the proportions of the room, certain types of pattern will appear over-frivolous. You may be unlikely to receive customers and visitors to your home office, or you may work within a creative industry which will appreciate such adornment; otherwise, try to retain a professional air within your work setting and select your colours and patterns in the same way you would your business card or logo.

Pictorial pattern can be used to great effect in the home office as it is in many other rooms within the home. In this setting, it is the perfect tool for creating a smart atmosphere that still retains a domestic feel, as it is more decorative than the traditional types of pattern associated with the office. So, a pictorial scheme can create the more personal, less formal working atmosphere that is desired by those who work from home.

Pictorial pattern need not be supplied only with wallcoverings and fabrics, of course. The easiest way of introducing pictorial detail to a room is to arrange real pictures on a wall. In the same way, a picture can be created from the way you arrange or display non-pictorial items such as books. Most studies and offices will have a good supply of reference books. The way these are displayed will undoubtedly have a great impact on the overall appearance of your room. If you wish to retain a strong decorative appearance in your study or home office, you must carefully consider your approach to the storage of such items. In a period property, for example, built-in shelving should be created in a style that is sympathetic to the age of the property. Large bookcases can also conceal high-tech items, such as computers and fax machines, behind false doors that have been cleverly manufactured and dressed with false book spines to emulate the rows of actual books displayed on either side. Avoid the over-use of items like false books though, as they will never replace the character and professionalism that is associated with the real thing.

Left: A SMALL AMOUNT OF PICTORIAL DETAIL CAN GIVE A WARM DOMESTIC FEEL TO THE MOST PROFESSIONAL WORKING ENVIRONMENT. HERE THERE IS PICTORIAL PATTERN IN THE PLACING OF THE PAINTING ON THE WALL, AND IN THE CURTAIN FABRIC WHICH IS USED ON THE REVERSE OF THE CURTAIN FOR A SUBTLER EFFECT. THE PICTORIAL ELEMENTS ARE INTEGRATED WITH THE REST OF THE ROOM THROUGH THE COLOURS. THE CURTAIN FABRIC LINKS TO THE CHAIR, AND THE BLUE IN THE PAINTING TO THE BLUE OF THE WALLS.

Right: UNLESS YOU ARE AN EXPERIENCED INTERIOR DESIGNER, TRY TO KEEP THE DECORATION OF YOUR HOME OFFICE SYMPATHETIC TO THE AGE OF THE PROPERTY. HERE TRADITIONAL BOOKCASES INTRODUCE DETAIL AND INTEREST, WHILE FAUX BOOKS HAVE BEEN USED TO CREATE A PICTORIAL EFFECT. HOWEVER, YOU SHOULD BE VERY CAREFUL NOT TO OVER-USE FAUX BOOKS AS AN EFFECT, AND LIMIT THEM TO SMALL AREAS.

Home Offices and Studies/*Texture*

The neutral-feeling schemes that can be achieved by introducing a range of textures, rather than colours, are perfect for the home office. Textures will provide depth and interest in any scheme, although in the office setting the emphasis should be on a combination that will stimulate rather than relax.

When selecting the materials for your working environment bear in mind the look you want to achieve, and the style of the rest of your home. For a mellow look, combine natural matting with distressed or aged timber furniture and softly colourwashed walls. Or, for a contemporary setting, try introducing harder, shinier materials which will create a sleeker finish. Consider combining elements such as smooth timber flooring, shiny metal and glass, set against a colourful backdrop.

Remember that the pattern inherent in the texture of a natural material, such as wool, wood, muslin or stone, replaces the need for any superimposed pattern. Allow nature to be your designer and you will create a room which is easy for anyone to work in. When considering soft furnishings or curtaining for the home office, look at woven fabrics incorporating a single-coloured pattern or design. In this context, they will be just as decorative and effective as any highly stylized or coloured material. Wooden and metal blinds are also a good alternative to traditional curtain dressings in the work setting. They not only allow light to be filtered according to your practical needs, when and how you want it, but also add a strong line of pattern to a room with their horizontal slats.

Think textural when it comes to your choice of wall-coverings too. Vinyl wallpaper is available with a raised surface, while hessians and other natural fabric wall-coverings extend the range available. Even painted walls can be given a strong textural finish now. Companies are producing paints that look like brushed denim and even suede, when applied in a cross-hatching motion. If you like to feel cosy and cocooned while you work, then warm-coloured textural finishes would be ideal.

The textural home office is the ideal place in which to experiment with alternative designs of storage too. Glass bricks and concrete blocks can be used to great effect within a contemporary setting to create simple but stunning shelving systems. Choose a material to contrast and complement the other textures and the natural tones in the room, such as shiny aluminium with mellow wood, or Perspex with fur.

Do not feel obligated to restrict yourself to neutral or natural colour schemes when producing a textural home office environment. Tactile surfaces like faux furs and natural matting can be set just as well against a vibrant background. If you work within an artistic field, it can be very rewarding to add details that demonstrate your artistic talent. Covering files and storage boxes with unusual fabrics is a simple way of expressing yourself in your home office environment. You do not have to conform to company regulations now, so a space used for working at home can be far more reflective of your personality and individual style and taste.

Above: A STYLISH AND MODERN SCHEME CAN WORK EQUALLY WELL IN A TRADITIONAL PROPERTY. HERE BLEACHED WOOD, ALUMINIUM, AND SILVER AND GREY PAINTWORK HAVE BEEN COMBINED TO CREATE A STYLISH YET PRACTICAL OFFICE WITHIN A PERIOD HOME.

Left: THE HOME OFFICE DOES NOT NEED TO BE LIMITED TO A CORPORATE STYLE OF DECOR. HERE TEXTURAL DETAILS SUCH AS RUSH MATTING AND ANIMAL PRINT FABRICS COMBINE TO CREATE A WARM AND WELCOMING AFRICAN-STYLE INTERIOR. IT IS A WONDERFUL WORKING ENVIRONMENT FOR AN ARTISTICALLY MINDED INDIVIDUAL.

Home Offices and Studies/*Plain Colour*

Blocks of individual colour are a useful tool for identifying a working space within a multifunctional room. A change in colour can denote a change of function within a decorative scheme, although you must be careful that the colour still works with the scheme as a whole, rather than isolating the area completely and making the space appear disjointed.

In a busy home, creating the space needed for an office is often difficult and requires a certain amount of ingenuity on behalf of the designer to identify and open out areas that may have previously been limited in their use. The home office featured here (right), for example, has been positioned within a glazed rear entranceway to a property. The area is very narrow. However, with clever planning, a desk and storage have been housed within an alcove on the internal wall. Notice how blocks of colour have been used in a controlled way to add character and depth to the space. Painting the whole area in a deep colour would only have emphasized its small dimensions, but using a single block within the alcove and a primary red on the chair has made the space more stimulating. In the day, the room benefits from a profusion of natural light, while in the evening, lighting is supplied over the main desk area, giving the colour even more impact. In a room such as this, the furniture chosen must be practical, yet not overpowering. The chair, for example, folds away when not in use, making the available floor area as serviceable as possible.

If you have a preference for contemporary styling, colour can play a key role in your home office scheme. Think about using blocks of individual colour to create a stylish and clear-cut interior. The modern study here (left) is given instant warmth and character from the uplifting shade of orange on the walls, which tones beautifully with a simple timber floor. The large painting plays a central part in the scheme, with its white background giving relief to the orange wall on which it sits, and introducing a block of contrasting colour.

Furniture too is very important to complete the look. There are many ranges of home office furniture now available, but a large proportion of them are of a traditional style. For a unique, alternative look, why

not consider how you might use products which were not originally designed for the study or office setting. In the small study featured here (left) a large desk would have overpowered the room. The designer has therefore created a stylish and practical alternative by making a table from two simple wooden trestles supporting a plain glass top. (Obviously care has to be taken when using glass as a table of any kind in a domestic setting, so ensure that safety glass of a suitable thickness is used.) Because this style of desk does not offer any drawers, ample storage space needs to be allocated elsewhere within the room.

Left: COLOUR CAN BE USED TO ADD LIFE AND VIBRANCY TO A SCHEME – AND IT CAN ALSO HAVE A GREAT EFFECT ON YOUR MOOD. IF YOU REQUIRE A SPACE IN WHICH TO STUDY AFTER A LONG DAY AT WORK, OR JUST SOME GENERAL MOTIVATION TO WORK, ORANGE WILL PROVIDE THE PERFECT UPLIFTING AND STIMULATING ENVIRONMENT.

Above: TAKE TIME TO CONSIDER DIFFERENT SPACES WITHIN THE HOME THAT MAY CURRENTLY BE WASTED. A GLAZED CORRIDOR ACTING AS REAR ACCESS TO THE HOUSE CAN EASILY BE CONVERTED TO PROVIDE THE PERFECT SPACE FOR A HOME OFFICE. WHEN GIVEN SOME CLEVER SPLASHES OF COLOUR, IT DEVELOPS A CHARACTER ALL OF ITS OWN.

3

THEMED
DECORATING

CONTEMPORARY
style

Many people find contemporary style hard and uncompromising. However, to its dedicated followers, it is an inspirational look that delights in the essential character of the materials used and their juxtaposition. In a contemporary colour scheme, wood is chosen for its beautiful grain, colour is used for its emotional and aesthetic impact, and metal is used for its crisp, gleaming, hard-edged qualities. All the products used are 'honest', chosen for their ability to undertake the function for which they were designed and introducing all-important textural variations.

Contemporary style is, unsurprisingly, the most fashionable and forward-looking style, but the ideals that form its backbone are not so modern. Charles Rennie Mackintosh designed his high-backed Hillhouse chair nearly one hundred years ago in 1901, yet it looks fitting in today's contemporary homes. Allowing form to follow function was the brief Mackintosh set himself and the same brief which inspires contemporary designers today.

The Arts and Crafts movement, which evolved in Britain in the early twentieth century, also believed in getting back to what was basic, useful and workable. Solid oak furniture, plain whitewashed walls and hand-crafted ceramics were its trademark – and they are all elements of contemporary style now, a century later. The American Frank Lloyd Wright, whose career ran from the late 1880s to the Fifties, exemplifies this. His interiors are Modernist, a benchmark for contemporary style throughout this century and yet they have Arts and Crafts elements.

Left: THE CONTEMPORARY INTERIOR IS A CLEAN-LINED ENVIRONMENT WHICH IS EASY ON THE EYE AND SOOTHING TO THE MIND, PERFECT FOR ESCAPING FROM THE RIGOURS OF MODERN LIVING.

Right: A CONTEMPORARY ROOM DOES NOT RELY TOTALLY ON COLOUR. TEXTURE AND NEUTRAL OR NON-COLOURS CAN BE USED TO GREAT EFFECT, AS IN THIS STYLISH BEDROOM.

Colours

Colours are used with purpose in this setting. Remember that less is more and choose your colours carefully – an indiscriminate use of colour will lose its power. Consider how the colour you choose will alter the aesthetic appearance of an area, or inject a certain atmosphere into the room.

While white is a predominant colour (or, indeed, non-colour) in this style, punctuations of colour add relief and interest to the scheme. If your scheme is not going to be a completely white and neutral one, your palette should be strong, bold and bright. The current trend is for secondary and tertiary colours – that is colours that lie between the primary colours on the colour wheel. Pure primary colours – that is bright red, yellow and blue – should be avoided nowadays, because, although they are bold and strong, they are too reminiscent of the Eighties' high-tech look. Today's contemporary-style interiors have a slightly softer edge.

In the main, contemporary colour schemes fall into the following categories: neutral schemes (using pattern or texture combined with white, cream, beige, caramel, brown and black); textural (where interest is created by

an emphasis on the contrasts between a variety of textural materials); complementary or contrasting (colours are chosen from opposite sides of the colour wheel, for example, orange and blue); and, finally, harmonious (colours appear combined with their neighbours on the colour wheel, for example, terracotta, red and orange or aquamarine, blue and lime).

Movements in fashion too have an effect on the colours chosen for the home. Watch how the colour palettes seen on the catwalk quickly find their way into our homes and so learn how to be one step ahead.

Fabrics and soft furnishings

Texture is a key word and soft furnishings are an ideal way of introducing this all-important element. Natural fabrics look wonderful in a contemporary room. Linens and cottons make beautifully simple window treatments and serviceable covers for upholstery, while rustic woven fabrics, waffle-weave cottons, leather and fur all make wondrous throws and cushions to scatter around a living room or bedroom. When you are making your selection, look to combine texture with a touch of self-indulgence to soften this often very ordered style.

Patterns have their place in a contemporary room, but should be used with reserve. The saying 'less is more' is once again true. A simple cushion in a desired pattern will sit more easily here and have a greater impact than a whole sofa and chair covered in the same fabric. When you are introducing pattern, opt for bold fabrics featuring strong graphic designs. Designs typical of the Art Deco movement are perfect.

So, if pattern is to be kept to a minimum, the colour of your soft furnishings will need to have some impact. Solid blocks of colour work well, so if you don't want to be neutral, be bold. Grass green, sunset orange and deep blue can all be used to add a touch of drama to a simple chair cover or an understated window treatment.

Walls

Paint is a popular finish for a contemporary setting, providing a flat, matt and unpretentious backdrop for the simple lines of the furniture. As all the emphasis is on the intrinsic qualities, such as the character and practicality of materials, dressing the walls with wallpaper seems a rather dishonest form of pattern. Instead, pattern is often supplied via specialist paint techniques, such as a simple but vivid colourwash, or gold and silver leaf applied in a random pattern to a pre-painted surface.

A plain, painted wall will make a bold decorative statement in its own right, but occasionally you will feel the need to provide some decorative interest. Framed pictures or abstract painted details can be positioned on a wall in such a way as to add pattern and movement to that surface.

Left: FOR CONTEMPORARY STYLE, TRY TO THINK UNCONVENTIONALLY BUT SIMPLISTICALLY, WITH AN EYE FOR FUNCTION. A GLASS BLOCK WALL ALLOWS LIGHT TO STREAM INTO THIS BATHROOM AND MAKES A STUNNING CONTRAST WITH THE SLEEK AND MINIMAL BATHROOM FITTINGS.

If you are moving or adding dividing walls, think beyond the obvious painted partition and consider the aesthetic effect of other materials as well. Brick, stone, wooden veneer and glass can all be used to add texture and detail, allowing you to treat space and room divisions in a more exciting and unconventional way.

Floors

There is a clean edge to the contemporary interior, a crispness that underlines the ordered yet soothing environment, so it is natural, then, that the floorcoverings for such a setting should also have a simple, clean edge. Hard flooring works extremely well in any room or area, from the living room to the bedroom. Vary your choice of finish by using mellow timber, slate, stone, hard shiny ceramic tiles or even painted concrete as a

foil to your contemporary scheme. For a hard flooring that will introduce some pattern, remember the geometric patterning offered by mosaics, or for a truly sleek and modern look why not use metal? Galvanized steel and aluminium sheets, normally seen with relief geometric patterns, are a perfect example of the utility style entering the domestic scene. Once the chosen flooring for a heavy industrial setting, they are now a stylish addition to the contemporary home.

If you still yearn for the comfort of carpet, then choose carefully. Thick, luxurious carpet pile adds to the sensual qualities of a contemporary setting, but this is not the place for a traditional pattern. Your carpets should either ooze colour to make a design statement or be neutral-coloured blocks of texture. Rugs also look wonderful in this setting, with geometric-based large scale and abstract designs working best.

Summing up the style

Left: IN A CONTEMPORARY SETTING, A SIMPLE USE OF COLOUR AND FORM CAN MAKE A STRONG STATEMENT, BUT ADD A TEXTURAL ELEMENT, AND THE IMPACT OF THE ROOM WILL BE MAXIMIZED.

1. Artwork can have a profound effect on a room. Here large canvases, featuring harmonious colours in a mixture of media, play a crucial part in defining the overall effect of the room.

2. Colour is used throughout in blocks. Large comfortable pieces of furniture introduce textural variation and colour to the room.

3. Lighting is very important in contemporary design. Not only should it offer a good range of practical light sources for reading, entertaining and so on, it should also create focal points around the room. Occasional lights in this setting are often works of art in their own right.

4. The design of each individual piece of furniture is very important in a contemporary setting. Each piece must earn its place. This very sculptured bird's-eye maple, veneered table introduces sensual curves which complement the sofa and contrast with the straight lines of the rest of the room.

5. The clean lines of this mellow timber flooring provide a perfect complementary background for the plush textural furniture.

COUNTRY HOUSE
style

All over the world, country house style is loved and copied, because of its ability to be both comfortable and practical, elegant and unpretentious, ordered and yet informal.

Country house style contains many classical references originating during the Georgian period which spanned from the mid-eighteenth century to the early nineteenth. Balance, order and symmetry are all important to this style of decoration. A room of this kind must provide a background that is easy on the eye, so balance is crucial to its success: panelled walls should be positioned in a way that they appear even, fireplaces should be centrally located, as well as grand and imposing (Adam-style fire surrounds are a perfect option), and the mantelpiece is carefully decorated with symmetrically positioned candlesticks on either side of a gilt overmantle mirror. Other architectural details, such as picture rails or decorative coving, are emphasized by their decoration in order to give the room a sense of history, anchoring it into period style.

The furniture seen in the country house is comfortable, but it is not uniformly matched. This is not the place for the three-piece suite, or even for a collection of furniture which suggests a particular fashion. Furniture should not fall into a specific period, but should give the appearance of being collected and added to over the years, handed down from generation to generation to create a personal yet eclectic blend that is relaxed and unpretentious. That said, achieving a successful country house look cannot be left to chance or a process of natural evolution. It takes great skill and planning to create a room that looks so utterly unmanufactured!

Right: COUNTRY HOUSE STYLE SHOULD APPEAR AS IF IT HAS EVOLVED OVER THE YEARS, WITH CHERISHED PIECES OF FURNITURE AND BEAUTIFUL YET PRACTICAL FURNISHINGS.

Above: THIS FRENCH-STYLE COUNTRY HOUSE BEDROOM IS ELEGANT AND RELAXING. IT COMBINES FADED FABRICS WITH PAISLEY AND FLORAL PRINTS TO CREATE AN ATMOSPHERE OF UNDERSTATED ELEGANCE.

Colours

The spectrum of colours used in the country house interior is very broad. Classical, refreshing colours like yellow, blue and shades of green have strong links with this style, while combinations such as warm peach, apricot and cream are ideal for creating a soft and welcoming interpretation of this look.

Colours are often faded in appearance as true colours can look too modern. One tip, from famous interior designer John Fowler, is to add a very small amount of black or grey to your paint colour to add a rounded softness to your chosen shade. Cream has long been used as a background colour for country house furnishings and eau de nil is another popular choice. Both of these colours are unassuming and timeless, and provide the perfect foil for an eclectic collection of faded furnishings and furniture.

Above right: IT IS NOT JUST THE SITTING ROOM THAT CAN BENEFIT FROM COUNTRY HOUSE STYLE. THIS ROOM HAS BEEN DESIGNED WITH THE TRADITIONAL COOK'S KITCHEN IN MIND. IT HAS NOSTALGIC CHARM, BUT OFFERS A STYLISH SOLUTION TO THE DEMANDS OF FAMILY LIVING.

you the ideal opportunity to introduce additional texture and pattern to the room.

Pattern-matching should be done with extreme caution. Avoid coordination, as it will look too contrived, but look instead to mix florals with stripes, checks and self-weaves. A number of different fabrics with a nostalgic feel can combine to create an atmosphere that appears to have evolved over the generations, giving a finished look that is relaxed and elegant, rather than city smart and over-designed.

When it comes to dressing your windows, however, you can throw caution to the wind and indulge yourself. Country house style originated at a time when curtain making was at its fore, and fine fabrics and elaborate curtain and window drapery techniques were thought to be the height of good taste. Use your curtain and window treatments to enhance the proportions of your room and soften the window edges. This

Fabrics and soft furnishings

A wide range of soft furnishings can be used in the country house setting, depending very much on the atmosphere required from the finished room. Damasks, brocades and fine silks in faded colours can look wonderfully elegant in these surroundings, whereas floral chintz and cotton provide an informal, fresher look, introducing the atmosphere of the country garden into the home. These last fabrics look best in the less palatial country house setting, but, while they may lack the grandeur associated with silks and damasks, they retain a charm that is very much central to this beautiful decorative style.

Upholstery fabrics can be made into casual loose covers, preferably washable, as they will no doubt need to cope with dog hairs and muddy paws! Layers of throws, blankets and cushions in a mixture of antique, worn, and newer fabrics provide a comfortable, informal finish while offering extra wraps when it gets chilly at night (country houses are invariably cold!). They also give

is not a style for hard lines or for minimalism. Choose generous amounts of fabric made into simply gathered pelmets for an understated country house style or opt for swags and tails and more elaborate window treatments to produce an opulent air. (Avoid using very angular window treatments like straight pinch pleat pelmets, however, as they will contradict the essentially informal setting and appear too modern.) If you are on a restricted budget, metres of curtain fabric might be too much of a luxury, so try combining roman blinds with dress curtains for a cost-effective, pleasing look.

Walls

In order to give your country house a sense of history and faded grandeur, traditional architectural details are essential. Plain plastered walls can be decorated with architectural mouldings such as decorative covings, picture rails, dados and panelling, to produce the desired effect, then paint these with a matt, eggshell finish. The surrounding wall areas can then be covered with either simple paint finishes or decorative wallpaper.

The wallpapers best suited to this style include smart stripes, softly distressed damask prints and classical-inspired patterns – although the more modern country house may feature decorative paint techniques such as dragged and ragged effects or colourwash finishes. The overall effect should be soft, faded and elegant, rather than sharp and smart.

Floors

In hardwearing areas, such as hallways and kitchens, hard, practical flooring – marble and stone – suits the style of the country house. Elsewhere the emphasis is on a combination of traditional style and comfort, so timber floors, such as parquet or simple, highly polished floorboards, look perfect, especially when rugs are used to add pattern and comfort. It is important, however, to retain a deep border of timber around the perimeter of the room for an unfitted look. Oriental or Aubusson tapestry rugs are perfect for the country house interior. One central rug will create a centre point around which to place your furniture, while a number of rugs placed around the floor will give the room a slightly more relaxed atmosphere.

Carpets, if used, could feature small, repeating, geometric patterns with deep decorative borders.

Right: WHILE THIS SITTING ROOM MAY NOT BENEFIT FROM THE GRANDEUR OF LARGER PROPERTIES, IT IS STILL ELEGANT, COMFORTABLE, RELAXED AND GRACIOUS – THE EPITOME OF COUNTRY HOUSE STYLE.

1. A simple, yet generous, curtain style is used here in a glazed cotton fabric – the floral pattern is ideal for a country house window overlooking a garden.

2. Striped wallpaper is used to create a traditionally formal country house atmosphere and add extra height to the walls.

3. The sofa has been covered with quite a modern upholstery fabric, but, topped with a mixed collection of decorative cushions and a throw, it can then be successfully incorporated as a modern addition to this traditional style.

4. A well-worn leather armchair brings a nostalgic air to this room, showing how antique, even shabby, pieces of furniture or furnishings are at home in country house decoration.

5. An upholstered footstool doubles as a coffee table. Footstools are a useful way of introducing some extra pattern and colour on a small scale, while their softness contributes to the overall informal look. They are also handy when an extra seat is needed.

Summing up the style

CLASSICAL
style

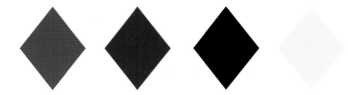

**Classical style is dedicated to achieving a harmony of proportion and detail.
Elegant and distinctive, its qualities can be applied in their purest form to
produce a definitive classical room, but it can also teach us lessons of balance
and reserve that are invaluable when developing other styles of interior.**

In historical terms, classical style was inspired by the art and architecture of ancient Rome
and Greece. Highly respected for centuries, it has been the basis for, among others, the
fourteenth- to sixteenth-century Renaissance, seventeenth-century Baroque, the early
eighteenth-century Palladian revival, and mid-eighteenth-century Rococo. Most of these
movements were worldwide.

Today we are surrounded by so many classical details, original and reproduced, that it is
easy to take them for granted. The Adam-style fire surround with its decorative motifs, the
columned doorways associated with Georgian properties and the geometric marble-clad
hallways of grand houses and hotels are all examples of classical styling that have already
lasted for centuries and still take a prominent place within modern decorative schemes.

However, classical style has become a term used to describe an eclectic blend of
decorative details, combined in an elegant and ordered interior. You no longer need to
recreate a historically accurate classical room, but can take elements of the style and use
them to create a certain ambience or effect. A room designed in a classical way has
symmetry and a strong sense of dignity and calm. In this century's classical room, marble
bowls, bronze Empire-style busts, columns, obelisks or sphinxes can all be displayed if you
wish, but the classical theme does not have to be carried through to the smallest detail.
Symmetry and architectural details featuring classical motifs can be surrounded by plain
fabrics and upholstery to create a contemporary setting supported by classical ideals.

Left: Here geometric flooring complements and restrains
the flowing trompe l'oeil drapery, while handpainted mural
work completes an unmistakably classical look.

Colours

The classical palette is very broad, as it is derived from so many classically inspired periods in history. The seventeenth century saw primary yellows and blues, together with shades of green and brown, in its interiors, while the first half of the eighteenth century was inspired by the white and gilt reception rooms of the late seventeenth-century French courts. (In those days, however, white was not the brilliant white we expect now. Less bright and powerful than our modern version, historical white was more of an off or dirty white.)

A softer classical effect can be achieved with the

perennially popular muted pinks, or the lighter shades of terracotta, grey, pearl, straw and Chinese yellow.

The bolder colourist may want to create a dramatic classical look by featuring Pompeian red (dark red terracotta) and black. This combination was inspired by Etruscan pottery, and has been widely used to evoke some of the warmth of a Mediterranean setting while maintaining the formality of the classical style.

Fabrics and soft furnishings

The classical look may be stylish, but it is far from fussy. Broad stripes in natural colours and monochrome schemes provide a perfect backdrop for classically inspired paintings and artefacts, especially in simple fabrics such as linen and canvas. If, however, you like the idea of something more colourful or extravagant, French Empire style is also perfectly at home in this setting. This style originated in late 1790s France and included Roman classical motifs; it allows you to splash out on silks, taffeta and moiré, and to introduce stripes in vivid yellow, bright green and crimson.

If you want to introduce a motif pattern, there is a wide range of fabrics decorated with statues or urns, all of which will make a strong graphic impact and help to create a distinctive classical interior. Look out for companies who specialize in classical-style fabrics. They will produce sheers, cotton satins and velvets in both black and white, and classical colours, every season.

Once you have selected your fabrics, give careful consideration to the style of your window dressings. The look is simple but sophisticated, allowing the lengths of fabric to emphasize the classical proportions of large, tall windows. Asymmetric-style drapery designs are commonly used on pairs of windows where the design is mirrored on the second window to create the look of one larger window dressing. This also adds an element of the symmetry associated with this style. In the more dramatic colour scheme, hang your curtains from black and gilt curtain poles or finish them with gilt pelmets. Or, for a pared-down version of classical style, muslins and sheers add a delicate touch to complement the paler palette.

Walls

Plain finishes and architectural detailing are the key to successfully decorating walls in this style. Neutral shades of colour-washed walls, sandstone-effect wallcoverings or faux paint techniques are perfect options for a more subtle scheme, while broad-striped wallpapers in classical colours (with or without the addition of gold metallic details) can be used to create a more opulent environment.

The simplest approach is often the most effective. While neo-classical, Grecian or empire-style patterns are all available on wallcoverings, I feel that overpowering a room with a theme removes some of its charm. Use classical motifs as subject matter for the odd piece of artwork or objet d'art instead. Its cautious application will result in a more tasteful interior.

Right: CLASSICAL-STYLE
INTERIORS CAN BE EITHER
UNDERSTATED OR HIGHLY
DECORATIVE. HERE STRONG
COLOUR AND BOLD USE OF
CLASSICAL MOTIFS AND
ARTEFACTS CREATE A
STUNNING HALLWAY.

1. Simple stencil designs can decorate the walls in this style. Here they feature the head of a Roman emperor.

2. The ornamentation which decorates both the mirror and the bookcase in this hallway is of a classical order.

3. The bright yellow seen on the walls of this stunning hallway is a traditional colour associated with classical Georgian interiors.

4. This console table displays a pair of sphinx bookends which sit either side of a classical urn-based lamp. This type of symmetrical display is very important in this setting.

5. Black and white geometric-designed flooring is a traditional and aesthetically pleasing floorcovering for this environment.

Above: THIS LIGHT AND
SPACIOUS LIVING ROOM
DISPLAYS THE IMPORTANCE OF
SYMMETRY IN THE CLASSICAL
INTERIOR. EVERY ELEMENT IS
BALANCED BY ITS OPPOSITE
PARTNER: THE BOOKSHELVES,
THE COFFEE TABLES, THE
SOFAS, WHILE THE CLASSICAL
STATUE ACTS AS THE CENTRAL
POINT OF THE ARRANGEMENT.

Floors

Hard flooring is the most successful for this look. Georgian-style timber flooring offers warmth, practicality and beauty, and stone and marble, although colder underfoot, also suit the look perfectly. Use them either in a simple single-colour finish or combine them with additional colours to produce geometric patterning on which to place furniture and furnishings.

Natural floorcoverings are a suitable alternative to carpeting and can also be used either with a plain jute binding or with an additional border pattern, such as a classical scroll or Greek key border, to draw the eye to the perimeter of a room, or to define an area within it.

Summing up the style

MEDITERRANEAN
style

Mediterranean style can be textured and nostalgic, bright and inspiring, or understated and romantic. Although extraordinarily diverse in its regional style, the Mediterranean atmosphere is always colourful, vibrant and unpretentious.

Many of us think of the Mediterranean purely as a holiday destination. Yet, despite being a region synonymous with the sun, sea and sand, its strengths extend much further than being a hot spot for tourists. The region spans so many cultural and geographically diverse areas, from Tuscany to Tangiers, that it has proved to be the inspiration for many designers and artists throughout history.

As with many regional styles, Mediterranean offers numerous colour and pattern palettes, depending on the exact location from which it is derived, its history, folklore and climate. In southern Spain, for example, local products such as terracotta and glazed ceramics are frequently teamed with Arabic motifs, 'magic' carpets and burnished brass and copperware. These had been introduced to Spain by the Moorish settlers, of Berber and Arabic descent, who arrived in AD 711 and ruled the country for hundreds of years thereafter. Generally, however, Mediterranean style epitomizes simple living against a backdrop of whitewash and bright colour. The emphasis is on practical, natural and hardwearing materials, combined to offer a comfortable retreat from the sun.

Left: THIS RUSTIC HALLWAY PERFECTLY ENCAPSULATES THE MEDITERRANEAN LOOK. TIME-WORN TERRACOTTA FLOORS COMBINE WITH AGED HANDPAINTED FURNITURE AND WARM EARTH-COLOURED WALLS TO CREATE AN ATMOSPHERIC ENTRANCE.

Colour

This is the style for the colour-lover. Whitewashed villages may be a prominent feature of the Mediterranean, but there will always be a splash of bright blue, a door in aquamarine or a wall colourwashed in terracotta.

In Provence, for example, the colours and light of southern France are reflected in the decorator's palette. Strong yellow sits perfectly with Provençal red, the colour of rich terracotta. This, in turn, combines with vivid blue and olive green. Meanwhile, the Greek palette strongly features bright electric blue with contrasting sun-bleached white. Even the shadows cast against row after row of white hillside dwellings introduce a blue-grey to the palette.

The Spanish palette combines many of the same colours as are featured in other regions. Bright blues

contrast perfectly with sunshine yellow, while terracotta, a colour and product used throughout the region, sits effectively with olive green and the blue and white of traditional Spanish ceramics.

To capture the essence of the Moroccan colour palette, look again towards the more earthy tones such as terracotta, yellow ochre and burnt umber as the basis to your colour scheme. Spice colours will also introduce character to a scheme, so try a turmeric yellow, warm cinnamon or rich saffron gold. In general, these colours will all combine successfully to produce a warm and welcoming Mediterranean colour scheme.

So bright is the sun in the Mediterranean that even the strongest of colours will soon fade on walls and woodwork, leaving behind a bleached, pastel version of the original hue, and a nostalgic patina of distressed timber. For this reason you should not restrict your colour choice to the brightest and most vibrant of shades, but consider including peachy pinks, faded terracotta and lavender blue.

Also, while white is used widely in certain Mediterranean palettes – in their natural setting – it is wise to avoid it in cooler climates. If you live in the northern hemisphere, the natural light is quite different from that of the south and will give white a grey, flat look which is not as vibrant or appealing as the sharp bright blue-white that is seen in a Mediterranean environment.

Fabrics and soft furnishings

Strong sunlight can be hard to compete with, bleaching the very life and colour out of most fabrics. For this reason, soft furnishings are kept to a minimum and, when used, are natural and fresh. For your choice of material, look to linen, cotton, canvas and wool – these are practical and durable fabrics, which are an essential part of Mediterranean style. This is not the setting for delicate silks or satins, even if your climate is not as generous with the sun.

For your patterns, again keep it simple. Cotton stripes in blue and white, or golden yellow and white, are seen everywhere, from the sunbeds on the beach to the awnings outside hillside villas, while floral motifs, interspersed with olive green foliage and featuring the fruits of the region, are very popular as well. Strong Moorish geometric patterns are also ideal for those of you who hanker after some extra detail, with embroidered patterns and small mirrored embellishments adding a little 'magic'.

The colours and patterns of the fabrics should echo those of the walls and the landscape, and bring a touch of sunshine into your home. When trying to capture the essence of this style, combine bold contrasting colours like Provençal red (deep terracotta red) and golden saffron yellow, for example, to recreate the warmth associated with the Moorish regions, and use fabrics with lemon or olive motifs to remind you of hillsides covered in lemon trees and olive groves.

Window dressings are basic, as the sunlight would ruin luxurious drapes. Many Mediterranean rooms only

Below: THIS CONTEMPORARY KITCHEN COMBINES MANY MEDITERRANEAN ELEMENTS. THE BEAMED CEILING, THE DISTRESSED AND COLOURWASHED FURNITURE AND A MOSAIC-STYLE STENCIL BORDER, GIVE THE ROOM MORE THAN A TOUCH OF MEDITERRANEAN STYLE.

have timber shutters, with simple lace or sheer fabrics to diffuse the bright light – as well as to keep out any flying insects. If you want to add some curtaining, keep the look simple and practical. Pelmets should be avoided and curtains should be light, with a basic pencil pleat or gathered heading attached to the plainest of iron curtain rails or poles.

Walls

The relaxed, unpretentious air of Mediterranean style makes simple colourwashed paint finishes ideal for this setting. They emulate the softly weathered effect of the strong sun on limewashed walls and handpainted frescos. The paint finish chosen should be totally matt, similar to traditional whitewash and distemper paints originally used in this region. Yellows, terracotta, lilac or soft lime green are good background colours and contrasting colours can be used to frame windows and door openings, adding additional interest in a simple, unfussy manner.

Ceramic tiles play a prominent role in the Mediterranean home, thanks to their cooling and practical qualities. Consider using them on the walls in the main living areas, as well as in the kitchen or bathroom. Contemporary mosaic designs look perfect in this setting, and there are many decorative border tiles with a Mediterranean design, such as a coloured scroll on a fresh white background, which can be used to edge walls and windows.

Floors

To achieve an authentic look, your floors should be clad in natural, hard floorcoverings such as terracotta, stone and ceramic. In their home climate these keep a room cool and can be swept free of dust and sand each day. If your concern is keeping your toes warm, rather than cool, you may want to add a few rugs. These would not be out of keeping with Mediterranean style, where the occasional rug creates a centre point around which to position furniture. Popular designs include kelims and Berber rugs in warm spice colours with geometric patterns, which are often sold in the markets and on the beaches of coastal regions of the Mediterranean. Rush matting also offers a practical and textural alternative.

If carpet is a necessity in your home, choose a natural-looking design, such as a sisal or coir.

Right: SPLASHES OF BLUE, ON A BACKGROUND OF SIMPLE WHITE AND NATURAL TERRACOTTA, ARE AN EASY WAY OF GIVING A ROOM A MEDITERRANEAN FEEL.

1. Timber beams feature a great deal in the Mediterranean style of architecture. Here they have been painted white, but they still make an impact on the room, giving it an unpretentious and slightly rustic feel.

2. The white walls and ceiling in this original Mediterranean room have the effect of creating a cool environment – the perfect escape from the heat of the burning sun. However, in colder climates the effect would be grey and unwelcoming. Use other colours from the Mediterranean palettes as an effective alternative.

3. Keep soft furnishings simple and natural. Cottons and linens make effective curtaining when attached to plain curtain poles.

4. Blue and white traditional ceramics act as the perfect accessory in this style. Not only do they anchor the room in this regional setting, they also provide additional pattern to the interior.

5. Terracotta tiles add an intrinsically Mediterranean feel to an interior. They are also surprisingly warm underfoot in a house that has central or under-floor heating.

Summing up the style

SCANDINAVIAN *style*

Scandinavian style draws on a mixture of decorative influences from Sweden's colourful history, making it a wonderfully atmospheric look. It combines contrasting elements, brings together old and new, and features nostalgic, homely items, yet the overall look is fine, fresh and elegant.

Sweden's national wealth has fluctuated greatly over the centuries, and this has made its mark on the country's sense of style. In the seventeenth century, following the 30 Years War, Sweden's affluence and political power attracted architects and painters from all over Europe to its royal court. They brought with them the splendid Baroque style and introduced it to the country's gentry, who chose to use it in a more reserved manner than other countries during this period. Later, as Sweden's fortunes floundered at the beginning of the eighteenth century, Rococo style was becoming fashionable. This suited the Swedish designers, as it was a lighter decorative form, with less gilding and more discreet textiles, which was appropriate for the more restricted budgets.

A combination of reserved Baroque and delicate Rococo began to emerge but the style was given a twist when, in the middle of the century, the Swedish East India Company introduced imports from the east. The vogue for chinoiserie began and oriental-style wallpapers and textiles became increasingly popular. The Swedish government set up a manufacturing office to encourage the production of many of the imported styles of product, and Chinese-inspired blue and white ceramics began to appear.

Left: Minimal furnishings and handpainted panels are very reminiscent of Swedish interiors. Bare floorboards and basic furniture are essential — fitted carpets and rich upholstery would create a completely different look.

Left: STENCILLED OR HANDPAINTED FLORAL DESIGNS ARE A FAVOURITE DECORATION FOR WALLS IN THIS STYLE. DELICATE AND RUSTIC, THIS IS A MORE MODERN INTERPRETATION OF THE DESIGNS INTRODUCED BY ARTIST CARL LARSSON IN EIGHTEENTH-CENTURY SWEDEN.

Right: THE CONTEMPORARY SWEDISH-STYLE BEDROOM IS REFRESHING AND RELAXING. SOFT, OLD WHITE HAS BEEN USED ON THE TRADITIONALLY PANELLED WALLS AND THE FURNITURE. COMBINED WITH BRIGHTER WHITE LINEN AND RED DETAILING, THE RESULT IS A TIMELESS COLOUR SCHEME.

The Scandinavian style, as we know it today, was beginning to emerge, but another element was still to be incorporated. In the late eighteenth century, Prince Gustav returned from the French court of Louis XVI to become king, and introduced the spacious light colours and formal air of neo-classical style to his native country. He combined this with the scrolling lines of Rococo that were already in fashion, to produce the Gustavian mix of glass chandeliers, fine furniture, symmetry and ribboned swags.

These, then, are the influences you need to consider when creating a Swedish Gustavian look in your own home – a sense of reserved Baroque, a touch of Rococo, some oriental detailing and neo-classical formality. However, Scandinavian style also reflects a charming domesticity, which is best depicted by Sweden's most famous artist, Carl Larsson, and his wife, textile designer Karin. His charming paintings of everyday life featured his family going about their daily activities in their own home in Sundborn. These works demonstrated how, if tailored, the elegant style of the Swedish gentry could work in more humble surroundings. Larsson combined handpainted wall panels with embroidered textiles, applied splashes of bright colour with simply painted decorative chairs, and transformed the simplest pieces of furniture into works of art by applying decorative panels of flowers and foliage. It is this combination of clear colours, pared-down grandeur and country simplicity that defines the Scandinavian style and makes it unique.

Colours

The colours used to create a Scandinavian style can be divided into two: the soft palette, synonymous with grand formal dwellings, and the rustic palette chosen by those living in a more rural setting, away from the influence of high fashion. The soft Swedish or Gustavian palette combines colours that are pale and chalky. Grey-white and pastels such as soft pink, clear soft green, lavender and corn yellow add delicate detail and elegance to an interior. The rustic palette, however, is stronger and more practical, offering a healthy, hard-working country feel to a room. Typical colours would be deep red, dark blue, mid-green and golden yellow.

Fabrics and soft furnishings

The fabrics featured in Scandinavian-style interiors are nearly always basic cotton or linen, perhaps with the addition of sheer fabrics for romantic swaged pelmets and to dress otherwise bare windows. It is this simplicity of fabric that makes such an effective contrast with the finely decorated walls and furniture.

The pattern you choose should also be simple. Pick out woven checks and stripes in blue, red, pale green-grey and soft yellow, combined with white or ivory. Fabric designs in multicoloured patterns are rarely seen.

If you fancy something softer, then delicate florals are fine, especially if used in a single-colour pattern, or perhaps combined with a stripe. The toile de Jouy, a single-coloured chinoiserie design, and other orient-inspired blue and white fabrics also look very much at home in this setting, adding fine detail to a scheme.

Historically, the grander properties would have included floral patterns in beautiful silk fabrics to dress the windows, but the Swedish love of simplicity has rejected such extravagance in favour of an unpretentious elegance.

Walls

The walls of Scandinavian-style interiors can be given a distressed paint finish, as a basic backdrop for delicate or rustic pieces of furniture, or they can be treated more decoratively with panels and stencilling to add further colour and pattern to a room. Either way, the overall effect should be one of simple sophistication.

Plain painted or distressed surfaces are often divided at dado level. Sometimes this is by a timber moulding, but in many rooms the moulding is replaced by a simple painted line. A painted or moulded panel is often then continued above dado height, creating the decorative wall finish very much associated with this style. These panels can be left as a simple division for the application of various coloured paints or they can be used as a framework around which flowing foliage and flowers can be painted or stencilled, for a distinctive touch of Scandinavian decoration.

In bathrooms and kitchens it is easy to add an authentic feel by cladding the walls in blue and white traditional ceramic tiles, combined with fresh white paintwork.

Floors

With much of Scandinavia covered in forest, it is natural that the first choice for flooring would be timber. New or reclaimed wooden floors look perfect in the nostalgic setting, but, whichever you choose, ensure a bleached and faded appearance by either liming or colourwashing the boards. Ash and beech are naturally pale, but the rich colours of some timbers would overpower the subtle hues and country character of this style and should be avoided.

In areas where you want more softness or pattern, add some simple linen or cotton rugs. The majority of these are made from a thick warp thread interwoven with a thinner, more delicate weft, to result in a textural geometric design. More rural settings feature homespun rag rugs, made up of small lengths of recycled fabric in cotton and linen.

Summing up the style

Left: THE WONDROUS BLENDING OF OLD WITH NEW, AND GRAND WITH RUSTIC, UNDERLIES THIS SIMPLE, ELEGANT INTERIOR, PROVIDING THE NOSTALGIA THAT IS TYPICAL OF SCANDINAVIAN-STYLE INTERIORS.

1. The Swedish love for the ornate can be seen even in the most humble of settings, shown here in the form of a crystal-embellished chandelier.

2. Simple sheer curtains drape effortlessly over brass poles to create a typically Scandinavian window treatment.

3. A traditional fine upholstery fabric has been used on the gilded chairs, featuring a blue stripe with delicate floral detailing.

4. The furniture is a mix of rustic painted chairs and ornate gilded pieces. This is a perfect example of the contrasting mixture of styles that combine to create Scandinavian interiors.

5. Soft, mellow timber floorboards create the perfect background for rustic rag, and textural woven rugs.

VICTORIAN
style

Victorian rooms displayed an indiscriminate mix of historical details, a heavy layering of patterns, solid furniture and an excessive amount of artefacts and general paraphernalia. Cosy and cluttered, it is a style which brings a welcoming air of familiarity to any room.

How does such an eclectic style emerge? The answer lies in the economy and lifestyle of the period. Period styles do not just emerge following the change of monarch. Favourite trends in design continue in some form, from one era to another, slowly adapting and evolving in reaction to economic advances and major historical events. While classic Georgian style remained popular in Britain and America into the Victorian age (1837–1901), a new confidence was sweeping the large towns and cities of Britain at the same time. The Industrial Revolution was offering financial rewards to the ever-growing middle classes, who in turn invested their new wealth in international travel, styles and artefacts.

Britain's new confidence also created an atmosphere in which the urge to create a new style was born. However, as with many eras driven by wealth rather than innovation and design, the architects of the period looked back into history to discover their direction in style. The result was primarily a Gothic revival with Elizabethan, Egyptian, oriental and Rococo styles all being included as design elements.

Left: Heavy upholstery fabrics, highly patterned carpeting and a flowing Arts-and-Crafts-style wallcovering typifies the late Victorian period. The conservatory beyond this sitting room is another common feature of the era.

Queen Victoria herself was a strong advocate of family values, and it became fashionable to use the cornerstone of every family – the home – as a status symbol and public display of prosperity. Interior decoration was to be used as the yardstick for one's personal wealth and cultural knowledge. Today, the key to style is 'less is more', but Victorians had a very different approach and enthusiastically embraced the idea of extravagant decoration. After all, why should a window be dressed with a single pair of curtains if you can afford to add elaborate pelmets, laces and blinds?

Towards the end of the century, there was to be a reaction against such over-indulgence, with a number of groups attempting to move away from this heavy style. Groups such as the Arts and Crafts movement, led by William Morris, and the Aesthetic Movement made their mark on architecture, but also on the design of furniture and interior decoration in general. The emphasis was on craftsmanship, and, although they adopted motifs such as peacocks, oriental cherry and apple blossom designs, and medieval symbolism, a simple, natural air prevailed.

However, it is the dark, patterned and cluttered rooms that have made a lasting impression and have come to represent what is known as Victorian style.

Colours

Colour preferences changed during the Victorian era. Early Victorian decor saw light colours, such as pearl white, soft pink and lavender, but towards the middle of the century, darker colours became popular – partly due to the invention of aniline dyes, but also because the richness associated with these colours was very much en vogue. Deep blues, acid dark greens, purples and mustard were all very popular.

Left: IF THE DARK COLOURS AND CLUTTER DO NOT APPEAL TO YOU, THEN TAKE THE ELEMENTS OF THE STYLE THAT DO. HERE CERTAIN ASPECTS OF VICTORIAN DESIGN HAVE BEEN DRAWN TOGETHER TO CREATE A STYLISH, YET MORE RESTRAINED, VERSION OF THIS HISTORICAL STYLE.

Walls

Deep skirtings, dado rails, picture rails and coving were inherited from the Georgian period, but were now used as a tool to display a wide range of colours and patterns. Above and below dado height, and even the picture rails, a different covering, colour or finish would be introduced. A more durable finish, such as Anaglypta or Lincrusta embossed paper, would be used on the lower sections of the wall, and more extravagant finishes displayed higher up. Damask designs, for example, were used for wallcoverings as well as fabrics during this period. Flowing florals, flock velvets, paisley and classical designs were all used indiscriminately within the Victorian interior, and three-dimensional, trompe l'oeil printed wallpapers were also particularly admired.

If floral fussiness is not to your taste, then simpler patterns are also suitable. Stripes in broad, single-colour repeats were used throughout the home, although designs featuring rows of striped foliage were also popular.

The Victorians had a great love of emulating products that were either expensive or difficult to obtain. This led to the introduction of a range of wallpaper borders that imitated braids and gilt detailing. These were used on top of mock-fabric wallpaper designs to give the illusion of the walls having been upholstered as opposed to papered.

Even the timber detailing, such as the dado or picture rail, could not be left in simple white. The Victorians preferred to use faux paint finishes to give these mouldings the appearance of expensive hardwoods, such as mahogany. Decorative coving was also treated in a very elaborate manner, with oil glazes applied and then rubbed off the surface to enhance its three-dimensional quality.

At the end of the century, the Arts and Crafts movement introduced a lighter touch. Their palette included ivory, pale grey, olive green, burgundy, rose, hyacinth and ebony for wood.

Fabrics and soft furnishings

If you love furnishing fabrics, this is the style for you. Layers of different fabrics were used to dress everything from windows to doorways, arches, tables and even mantelpieces. The Victorian era favoured a wide range of materials and designs. Floral-printed chintz, featuring a variety of home-grown and oriental flowers, including the well loved rose, was used for both private and public rooms. Smaller repeat patterns were also popular: fleur de lys, scrolling leaves and heraldic motifs enhancing the Gothic feel, while acanthus leaves, swags and classical urns retained the classical air. Paisley and oriental designs were also popular.

For upholstery and soft furnishings, both woollen and silk damasks were used, while for curtains, velvets – both textured and sculptured – were combined with heavy fringing and tassels to create elaborate, and sometimes overpowering, styles. Window treatments were generally layered, however, featuring not only curtaining but decorative pelmets and valance designs, fussy blinds and lace panels.

Above: IF YOU DO NOT HAVE
THE TIME OR INCLINATION TO
SEARCH OUT ORIGINAL
FIXTURES AND FITTINGS, THEN
THERE ARE PLENTY OF
VICTORIAN REPRODUCTIONS
NOW AVAILABLE – ESPECIALLY
FOR BATHROOMS. HERE IS THE
PERFECT EXAMPLE OF A
VICTORIAN-STYLE BATHROOM
PRODUCED TODAY.

Floors

Hardwood timber flooring featured throughout the
Victorian period, so an easy way of recreating the style
is to strip and varnish old floorboards and top them
with a patterned rug. Carpets were also used widely,
though, with bordered floral designs, oriental-style
detailing and elaborate combinations of geometric patterning being popular.

The Victorian hallway had a mixture of both carpeting and hard flooring. The entrance hall was normally
clad in either black and white or encaustic ceramic
tiles, featuring geometric patterns and borders in beige,
brown, burgundy, green, blue, white and cream. These
were often complemented by carpet designs laid as run-
ners on staircases and secured with decorative brass
stair-rods.

Quarry tiles and flagstones were often seen in working areas below stairs, occasionally dressed with simple
and practical oil cloth rugs. In the late nineteenth century, linoleum became available and replaced these
high-maintenance stone and ceramic floors.

Right: IF YOU ARE A
SENTIMENTAL PERSON WHO
CAN NEVER THROW
ANYTHING AWAY AND LOVES
TO BE SURROUNDED BY ALL
YOUR TREASURES, THEN
YOUR IDEAL ENVIRONMENT
WILL HAVE A CLUTTERED,
NOSTALGIC STYLE SUCH AS
THE VICTORIANS CREATED.

1. This broad-striped, deep red
wallcovering is typical of the
Victorian period. It adds drama
and warmth to the usually
generously proportioned rooms
of the period.

2. Elaborate window dressings
are another recognized
feature of this period. Here,
paisley fabric has been ruched
to create a simple swag and
tail pelmet. The addition of
decorative fringing, ornate
tassel tiebacks and an extra
layer of heavy lace makes it
unmistakably Victorian.

3. The Victorians' love of
mixing patterns and colours is
perfectly demonstrated on this
traditional brass bed. Two
paisley designs combine with
traditional tartans, white
bedlinen and a woven
oriental-inspired fabric.

4. Very rarely is a space left
bare within the eclectic
Victorian interior. Every
available surface displays a
wide range of paraphernalia
and ornaments.

Summing up the style

KITSCH
style

Kitsch style has had a cult following for a number of years, but it has now outgrown and extended beyond that to become a great source of inspiration for fashion, interior design, graphic art and television. Now that such images are being seen by the public at large, kitsch is on the verge of an extraordinary revival.

Kitsch is a word with its origins in the Austrian vernacular expression 'Verkitschen etwas', which means to produce something that is sickeningly sentimental. Defined as 'worthless pretentiousness in art' in the dictionary, it has become synonymous with bad taste. As early as 1933, Herman Broch commented that all periods in which values decline are kitsch periods. However, these 'values' are highbrow perceptions of taste and style. Kitsch is only bad taste in the sense that it disregards this traditional ordered approach to design and does whatever it wants, with the emphasis on comfort, innovation and irreverent fun. The result is a style which is bold and colourful, with decoration everywhere and anywhere, and an unashamed sentimentality.

Historically, kitsch style can be seen throughout the twentieth century, but it has strong links with the Fifties, when mass culture really took off. The end of the Second World War gave people a renewed confidence and a zest for life. Rock'n'roll was all the rage; the Americans were doing everything bigger and better than before, and their new style was introduced to the world via their booming film industry. Everybody saw the American style, and, with mass-production, now everybody could have it.

Left: MANY CRITICS OF KITSCH FEEL THAT THE TYPE OF DECORATION IS NOT ALWAYS IN KEEPING WITH THE FUNCTION OF THE ITEM DECORATED. WHILE FLOWERS LIKE THIS MAY NOT ORDINARILY DECORATE A TOILET, WHY NOT?

The consumer era was upon us. It was an exciting period, especially in domestic design, where innovative products and designs were readily available. Brand-new materials like Perspex, melamine and Formica were being used for the manufacture of furniture. Colour was everywhere; and plastic was used to produce everything from upholstery to ornaments. There were colourful imitation flowers on the window sill and wine decanters covered in threads of coloured plastic in the drinks cabinet. Kitsch had arrived!

Colours

Blocks of confident colour combine in the kitsch style of interior – this is not a palette for the fainthearted. Deep red, mid-blue, bright yellow, rich purple, strong aquamarine and bright pink are the mainstay of all kitsch colour schemes, with popular colour combinations including red, black and grey; or red, lime and black.

Fabrics and soft furnishings

This style has a lighthearted approach to fabrics. Pictorial prints featuring joyful scenes, such as small children at play or even seated happily on their potty, were popular in the Fifties. Pets were also featured, especially the black poodle. Stylized vases and designs featuring fruit and vegetables were used in kitchens and dining areas alike, while the launch of Sputnik in 1957 gave the population a taste for space-age designs.

Kitsch fabrics often feature not just one pattern, but layers of patterns. Polka dots are commonly seen, not alone, but as a background to other stylized patterns, or combined with traditional floral designs in a frivolous version of the Victorian favourite. Less ardent followers of fashion in the Fifties felt that mixing the different patterns resulted in poor taste, but this did not dissuade fans, who were very happy to mix and match designs throughout their interiors.

Left: Many people associate kitsch with bad taste, but this is a very stylish kitchen. A soft pink provides a subtle backdrop for a wonderful collection of traditional appliances and free-standing larder cupboards dating back to the Fifties. The occasional modern piece fits into the style perfectly.

Above: Kitsch style has long been associated with the consumer-driven 1950s. This kitchen features the bright and bold colours of that era and the washable upholstery fabric which emerged then.

Technological advances brought wipe-clean furnishings to the home. These were seen as a revelation and were used widely in both furnishings and fashion. A range of tactile upholstery fabrics was also developed, which complemented the new simple but stylish furniture. In today's kitsch style, textured and boucle weaves work as the perfect upholstery fabrics, with faux furs and crushed velvets adding a touch of American ostentation to the interior.

Many original fabrics can be found in secondhand shops and car boot sales, although they are becoming more and more desirable, and designer versions of the furnishings from that period are now reaching ever-increasing values in the auction houses.

Kitsch window dressings are simple in style, if not in pattern. The Fifties interior featured sill-length curtains, dressed only by small pelmets or valances. No tie-backs were used, apart from in the occasional kitchen setting. Heavy lace panels also give a window an authentically kitsch look.

Walls

Architectural detail such as picture and dado rails do not feature in the kitsch interior, leaving the walls a blank canvas for large blocks of colour or patterned wallpaper. Vinyl coverings were being introduced to wallpapers in the Fifties, creating a range of very popular washable papers in geometric patterns, faux stone or wood panelling effects. Lovers of pictorial pattern were also indulged, with designers creating distinctively humorous wallcoverings depicting, for example, fruit and vegetables, cutlery and crockery.

Floors

Flooring does not escape pattern in the kitsch home. Simple, yet bold, geometric patterns are combined with blobs and thin chain designs to create Fifties-style carpeting. Plain carpets in bold colours include details such as fine non-parallel lines, adding a textural pattern to their surface.

Consider creating your own patterns by using carpet tiles in different combinations of contrasting colour, or you could design your own pattern for linoleum flooring. Now enjoying a huge comeback, linoleum was so popular in the Fifties that its use was extended beyond the kitchen, hall or bathroom to the bedroom as well.

Right: THERE IS SOMETHING LIBERATING ABOUT A KITSCH SCHEME. THIS IS BECAUSE YOU RID YOURSELF OF THE CONSTRAINT OF 'TASTE', SO YOU DO NOT HAVE TO FIT INTO ANY SPECIFIC STYLE AND CAN MIX AND MATCH AS YOU LIKE. HERE, ECLECTIC TREASURES, FIFTIES FURNITURE AND BRIGHT, BOLD USE OF COLOUR CREATE A SELF-INDULGENT HAVEN FOR THE KITSCH ENTHUSIAST.

1. While colourful plastics were very popular, gilt decoration was still featured in the Fifties. Plastic and plasterwork that has been painted gold is very much part of the kitsch interior.

2. Narrow display shelving is adorned with little ornaments of all shapes and sizes. This way of displaying your kitsch treasures has strong links with the Fifties too.

3. Faux fabrics and animal print rugs add to the fun atmosphere. The contrasts are startling, but it's not a style to be taken seriously.

4. Colourful melamine-topped thin-legged coffee tables are truly kitsch and work well with the curvaceous chairs of the same period.

Summing up the style

COUNTRY COTTAGE
style

Nostalgic, unpretentious and homely, country cottage style draws informally on a mismatch of furniture and traditional furnishings, and delights in the relaxed display of everyday objects. As so often happens with decorative styles, elements associated with the country cottage have crossed over into other decorative themes and help create today's casual lifestyle.

It is a style born out of necessity – as with most small properties, cottages lack sufficient storage space and leave the occupant no option other than to hang measuring jugs from the beams in the kitchen or store everyday crockery on open plate racks. It is this simple approach to living and the unpretentious air that makes this such a charming decorative style.

If you live in a modern apartment or town house, this is not the style to embrace in its entirety. It really works best in its natural surroundings – stone-built cottages with low ceilings and inglenook fireplaces, rambling old farmhouses with uneven flagstone floors, and pretty fishermen's cottages set off the cobbled streets of a coastal village are all natural homes to this look. That said, the country cottage style is still imitated in part by many people in their homes, regardless of the particular architecture. The use of unchanging and timeless soft furnishings, together with the roar of a natural log fire, is irresistible to many, and in the frantic technological era in which we live today, this relaxed style can be the perfect antidote.

Left: THIS NOSTALGIC BEDROOM INCLUDES MANY ELEMENTS OF COUNTRY COTTAGE STYLE. HOME-SPUN SOFT FURNISHINGS, SIMPLE WINDOW TREATMENTS AND COUNTRY FURNITURE CREATE A LOOK THAT IS FRESH AND TRADITIONAL, BUT NOT TOO 'TWEE'.

Below: A COUNTRY-STYLE KITCHEN WHICH IS BRIGHT AND INVITING, WITH MANY TRADITIONAL QUALITIES. IN FACT, THE SENSE OF HISTORY HAS BEEN SO WELL CAPTURED THAT, IF THE FRIDGE HAD BEEN HIDDEN BY A GATHERED CURTAIN OR CUPBOARD FRONT, IT WOULD BE HARD TO TELL THAT THIS KITCHEN WAS PART OF THE MODERN WORLD.

When trying to achieve a true country cottage style, look to the past for your inspiration and try to conceal any evidence of modern technology. Traditional details, such as beamed ceilings and open fires, are a must, and focusing on natural materials will help disguise any essential additions to the home. Antique-style pine kitchen cupboards, for example, could disguise the fridge, while the washing machine could be hidden under a simple cotton checked curtain. This is no place for polished stainless steel sinks. Instead, search out either originals or reproduction alternatives, such as a traditional Belfast (Butler's) sink.

Colours

Be inspired by the countryside and choose colours from the garden. Earthy tones, such as peach and terracotta, create a warm and inviting atmosphere and can be lifted by an accent of grass green or sea blue.

Above: THIS COTTAGE INTERIOR HAS A SLIGHTLY TEXTURAL RUSTIC FEEL TO IT, DUE TO THE TRADITIONAL TAPESTRY CUSHION COVERS, THE SIMPLY CRAFTED WOODEN FURNITURE AND THE WROUGHT IRON ACCESSORIES. THIS SCHEME PERFECTLY DEMONSTRATES THAT COUNTRY COTTAGE STYLE NEED NOT BE OVERLY PRETTY OR FUSSY.

Alternatively, opt for the shades of a spring flowerbed, using a soft sunshine yellow for walls and a delicate rose pink, lilac, bluebell and/or moss green for furnishings. Lack of natural light is a common problem for people who live in cottages, due to the small windows and low ceilings. So, to get the effect you want, you may need to choose colours that are slightly more powerful than normal, although not too bright. Acidic colours are too modern and contrived for this environment. Use yellows that are warm and quite powerful, but avoid citrus colours such as bright lemon, as they will look too synthetic.

Fabrics and soft furnishings

Again, be inspired by nature. Full-blown floral chintz or pretty rosebud-covered cottons are perfect patterns for the cottage home, but if you are not a fan of flowers, choose fabrics with a country association, such as tartans or tweeds. Look for natural fabrics with a home-spun look – this is not the setting for bright satins or silks, but for subtle and faded colours, or 'tea-stained fabrics', as they have become known. Choose traditional ginghams, designs which give the impression that they have been in the family for years, or combine antique textiles with new so that the join between old and new appears almost seamless.

Curtain styles are normally very simple, with nothing more than a gathered fabric pelmet above the window or just a basic wooden pole. Wrought iron poles are another alternative which look great, especially when combined with light clip-on headed curtains. If your windows are draughty you will need to stick to heavier, lined fabrics, but a lighter, blowsier look is ideal if you can get away with it.

Sofas should be covered in natural fabrics, such as cotton and linen, in a soft, unstructured shape. Washable loose covers are a practical choice for country living and suit the relaxed and comfortable style. Combine casual throws and woollen blankets with a jumble of different cushions to complete the look on sofas, chairs and antique beds.

Walls

Stone-walled cottages have a rough, uneven finish that is all part of the charm, so don't worry if your walls are not perfect. That said, do not try too hard to artificially recreate a rough plastered look. It can look very contrived and spoil the naturalness of this style. Adding false beams is something else to approach with great caution – you don't want your home to end up looking like a mock Tudor olde English pub.

That said, timber panels positioned below dado height can look very good in this style of interior. Try attaching the panels in a slightly uneven manner for really authentic rustic charm – although good joiners and carpenters may find this hard to achieve as it goes against everything they have been taught!

Any timber that is not left in its natural state should be painted, in either eggshell or traditional matt flat oil paints, as gloss or satinwood finishes are too shiny and modern-looking for this style. The walls themselves can be painted or papered. Plain painted matt walls are fine, but if you fancy adding some textural interest with a special paint effect, keep the pattern casual to prevent the room looking too 'designed'. For a really authentic feel, you could paint the walls with a traditional distemper or limewash. Wallpaper patterns also need to have a home-spun, traditional air. Look at simple stripes, rosebuds and trellis designs used in a small scale to suit the proportions of your rooms, which are likely to be limited.

Floors

Hard flooring, such as slate flagstones and quarry tiles, looks great in this environment and you can always throw down a few rugs in the areas that require some extra warmth or comfort. Your rugs can be anything from oriental to simple rag or oil cloth designs, as long as they don't look too modern. For this reason it is worth staying clear of fitted carpets, although natural flooring, like sisal and coir matting, is a good rustic-looking alternative. Today you can buy natural flooring materials, such as coir or sisal, interwoven with wool and other threads, for a softer, more decorative floor-covering.

Right: A COUNTRY COTTAGE INTERIOR NEED NOT BE CAUGHT IN A TIME WARP. CONTEMPORARY ELEMENTS AND PERSONAL PREFERENCES IN ART AND FURNISHINGS CAN ALSO WORK SUCCESSFULLY IN A COUNTRY COTTAGE ENVIRONMENT.

1. Built-in features such as this alcove storage unit should be kept as simple and plainly decorated as possible.

2. Beamed ceilings add to the atmosphere of the country cottage, but can be overpowering. Be cautious about adding mock beams to your home. Here the beam is painted the same colour as the ceiling to lessen its impact, but maintain its character.

3. Choose chairs and sofas that are large and comfortable. Soft furnishings should not be too colour coordinated, as the air should be one of comfort rather than planned decorative order.

4. A roaring log fire introduces warmth and a basic feeling of homeliness to this welcoming style of interior.

5. Rugs can be used to soften hard flooring, such as concrete, quarry tiles and flagstones, and add extra pattern and colour.

Summing up the style

GEORGIAN
style

The Georgian era spanned about 100 years from 1714 and has had a great effect on the way many homes are planned and decorated today. Elegant and timeless, it combines symmetry and order in a simple, yet sophisticated, manner. At the time, it was extremely popular in the whole of Europe, and, from the 1740s, in America too.

George I came to the throne in England in 1714, and from this time onwards, many domestic properties in large British cities were designed and constructed incorporating the ideals of a sixteenth-century Venetian architect, Andrea Palladio. This eminent architect was the author of *Quattro Libri dell'Architettura,* a detailed study of the ruins of ancient Rome. Palladio's study was translated into English in 1715 and revived classical style by classifying its elements into five orders of architecture – Tuscan, Doric, Corinthian, Ionic and Composite. This single work had a significant impact on architecture in the eighteenth century in Britain, Europe and America, from the large public buildings and grand houses like the Queen's house in Greenwich, England, designed by Inigo Jones, down to the average houses of the time, which incorporated basic stylistic details such as sash windows, entranceways featuring pilasters and columns, and pediments with semi-circular fan lights.

Left: THE SOFT COLOURS FEATURED IN THIS BEDROOM ARE PERFECTLY IN KEEPING WITH THE GEORGIAN PERIOD AND ITS SENSE OF RESTRAINED ELEGANCE. HERE THE FOUR-POSTER BED, WINDOW DRESSING AND STRIPED WALLPAPER EMPHASIZE THE GRAND PROPORTIONS OF THE ROOM, WHILE THE ARTWORK BALANCED AROUND A MIRROR ADDS THE ELEMENT OF SYMMETRY.

Robert Adam was one of England's most successful architects towards the latter part of the eighteenth century and was mainly responsible for the introduction of architectural detail to the interior. Following his lead, most Georgian properties featured plinths, classical pediments and pilasters as internal decorative details, as well as external features. He also devised a softer classical style by introducing Greek architectural themes to the previously Roman-based style. This neo-classical approach featured a delightfully delicate range of motifs such as classical urns, Greek key patterns, mythical beasts, scrolls and swags.

Georgian style, as we know it now, is not purely a product of classical or Palladian style, however. Rococo, originating in France, became popular in England at the start of this period, and introduced the Georgians to asymmetrical lines featuring scrolls and shells, together with other motifs derived from the delicate, curved line. Trade with the east was also opening up and this inspired a fascination with all things oriental. At the same time, Britain was experiencing a Gothic revival which was responsible for the introduction of the Trefoil and Quatrefoil motifs (made up of three or four overlapping circles) and the pointed arch. As a result, it was not long before some elements of all of these fashions merged together to create the look that we call Georgian today.

Colours

Georgian style is commonly associated with soft, pale colours, but inevitably, for a style encompassing a 100-year period, the palette changed and developed as time went on. The colour choice for the early part was a collection of darker earthy tones, muddy brown, pea green and eau de nil, all known as 'drabs'. Technological advances in paint manufacture eventually made way for brighter, paler colours in the second part of the century, so pink, light terracotta, pale green and Chinese yellow also suit the Georgian look.

Left: Elegant interiors were not confined to the grander properties of this period. Simple details such as the painted wall panelling and a traditional Georgian window give this more humble property a sense of the original style.

Below: The soft green walls featured in this Scottish Georgian house are typical of the period. Classical references are also to be seen in the decorative frieze and the Adam-style fire surround.

Fabrics and soft furnishings

The elegance of the Georgian interior was greatly enhanced by a wonderful range of soft furnishings. Rich fabrics, such as velvet, brocade, linen and silk damask, were widely used, while finer fabrics such as French and English floral chintz, silks, embroidered fabrics and toile de Jouy added a delicate touch to the interiors of many properties.

Fine woven silks and brocades displayed classical patterns such as urns and Roman motifs (inspired by Robert Adam) and, following major archaeological discoveries, together with plant-based patterns such as the acanthus leaf, scrolling foliage, trellis and lattice work.

A wide range of window dressings were seen, but all were elegant and some had a theatrical edge. Swag and tail pelmets with a very tailored design were prevalent, both with and without coordinating curtaining, while festoon blinds, suspended from ornate gilt pelmets, framed wooden shuttered windows.

Walls

Milk paints produced from skimmed milk and lime, with natural pigments supplying colour, were cheap and durable and were widely used on both plasterwork

and woodwork. They dry to a soft sheen, not quite matt and far from glossy, and are said to produce colours that have opacity and clarity – something that has been lost in modern manufacture, although it is still made today by specialists.

In the more opulent homes of this time, wallpapers were becoming widely used. Flock- and floral-designed damasks and chinoiserie-style papers featured regularly throughout the Georgian period (and are still easy to find today), while later on in the eighteenth century, floral-designed wallpapers bound with ribbon became en vogue.

Walls often featured classical-style panelling with vertical dimensions reflecting the elevated proportions of the architecture and echoing the profile of a classical pillar. The panels usually consisted of a skirting, a width of timber decorated with a moulding below the dado (chair rail), then the dado moulding itself, above which sat another raised panelled detail. This was all finished with an architrave that led into a frieze, and then an ornate timber cornice where the wall met the ceiling. This form of decoration was very expensive, and was therefore only seen in grander properties. However, a pared-down version without the upper panelling was also common elsewhere. To create the look yourself, prefabricated mouldings are readily available and look fantastic when painted the same colour as the walls.

Floors

Hard flooring provides an elegant and practical finish to the Georgian room. Stone and marble, featuring dramatic geometric designs, were used to decorate the floors of grander areas within the Georgian home, while general living rooms were enhanced by the wide use of mellow timber flooring – the perfect foil for the beautiful oriental-inspired rugs which were popular at the time. If you prefer to carpet your home, don't worry – carpets were also becoming more popular. In 1740, the Earl of Pembroke gave his patronage to the Wilton factory in England and throughout the country there was an upsurge in carpet manufacture. For a typical Georgian look, try to pick out a carpet featuring classical detail and edged with a complementary border. And, for a more authentic feel, avoid the completely fitted look and keep some timber exposed around the edge of the room.

Right: THE GEORGIAN STYLE IS WIDELY REVERED TODAY AND LOOKS JUST AS FRESH AND COMFORTABLE NOW AS IT DID IN THE EIGHTEENTH CENTURY.

1. The tailored lines of this swag and tail window treatment are accentuated by simple trimmings, and suit an elegant Georgian window.

2. The wall decoration featured here is typical of the Georgian period. A deep skirting, dado rail, panel mouldings and ornate decorative coving add a classical air to the room.

3. While contemporary furnishings, such as that on the fender, are used to great effect here, authentic fabrics, such as the damasks on the sofa cushions, are an essential link with the past.

4. Balance and order is very important in this environment. The console tables, classical lamps and decorative gilt mirrors on either side of the chimney breast add a classical symmetry to the room.

5. A beautiful oriental-inspired rug creates the centre point for the furniture layout in this elegant sitting room. An authentic Georgian atmosphere is created by exposing some timber flooring around the perimeter of the room.

Summing up the style

ORIENTAL *style*

The orient covers such a vast area that to classify the wealth of styles within it under one such heading is rather simplistic. However, there are common threads running through looks as distinct as Chinese and Japanese that clearly evoke a sense of oriental style. These include an appreciation of natural materials, a sense of order and an air of calm.

Oriental style has been an inspiration in interior design for centuries, with the Georgians in England and the Gustavians in Sweden among the wide range of people enchanted by its mystery.

Japanese interiors are calm and contemplative, with a sense of spirituality. The general structure of their interiors is based around a geometric order and there is little in the way of ornament, pattern or even furniture; and yet the finished effect is far from harsh. The emphasis on order and the quality and texture of natural materials creates its own interest and pattern: handmade rice paper, for example, stretched across geometrically designed interior windows and partitions diffuses the light in an attractive way, while bamboo and natural matting adds texture to floor surfaces while creating distinctive, angular patterns.

The Chinese also respect natural materials and a minimalist approach to furnishings, but to that they have injected a love of jewelled colour and pattern. Colours such as red, black and vivid blue combine with gold to make a more lively interior, decorated with lanterns, kites and oriental wood carvings. We can draw upon all of these influences to create our own oriental-inspired interiors.

Left: This unmistakably Chinese-inspired flamboyant bedroom features handpainted panels with oriental motifs and stunning opulent furnishings.

Colours

In Japanese interiors, mellow tones of wood and bamboo combine with the soft colours, such as off white, subtle stone, pale grey and parchment, which are seen in the delicate internal screens. Black and red lacquerwork can punctuate the scheme, but the overall palette is natural and calming, with bamboo greens and soft creams forming its basis. For a touch of Chinese influence, you can allow yourself some splashes of bright contrasting colour in your accessories or cushions.

Fabrics and soft furnishings

Natural fabrics in their original colours, or in black and white, suit the serenity of the understated oriental scheme, where fabrics actually have a minimal part to play. Cane blinds or shutters fit the clean lines of this style better than great swathes of fabric, and wooden furniture is left unadorned to let the beauty of the grain and form remain prominent. Your only fabrics, then, might be a blanket to throw over a futon, or some scatter cushions on your sofa.

If you feel your room does need some softening with fabrics, then keep it plain, or look for designs incorporating oriental calligraphy or graphic style motifs in appropriate shades. Windows would normally be left undressed, but you could hang a panel of sheer muslin, or a pair of very simple curtains. For a more elaborate look, there is always a good range of appropriate pictorial patterns, featuring bamboo, peacocks, dragons, lions, oriental warriors and delicate oriental ladies, with which to create sumptuous bed dressings or wallhangings.

An alternative approach would be to take the oriental porcelain designs as your inspiration and create a blue and white scheme with an unmistakably oriental touch, but with a softer finish.

Walls

How you decorate the wall surfaces of your oriental-style room will set the tone for the rest of the scheme. Chinese-inspired rooms can feature flamboyant and highly detailed panels, depicting intricate scenes of oriental life or imagery. Many of these are set upon a

Above: This opulent property features carved oriental furniture and ornate Chinese-inspired panels. It's a decorative look that few could replicate in its entirety, but which can offer inspiration for everyone.

Right: The minimalistic look of the Japanese interior is perfect for contemporary schemes. A dark wooden floor with inlaid squares of carpet echoes the grid of the shutters, while the texture of the grass cloth on the wall contrasts with the chrome spiral staircase.

black background, reminiscent of the black laquerwork furniture, and if used over a large area create a very dramatic and opulent look. If you are cautious about using so much pattern, then try introducing it perhaps on one wall only, or even on a removable wall, such as a decorative screen. This will help to create a feature out of a particular area without dominating the scheme.

The antithesis of this is the neutral walls of the more minimal Japanese interior. Plain neutral paint is ideal, or, for a softer look, a paint effect or paint-effect wallpaper is an alternative. Hessian and woven wallcoverings made from natural grasses are more popular again now, thanks to renewed interest in texture, and are perfect for the oriental-style room. If you are keen to experiment with different textures, then why not take a tip from the Japanese and try mixing some tiny pebbles or shells into the plaster finish on your walls? This will give a rough, tactile finish. An alternative is to mix some texture, such as sand, into your emulsion paint before you apply it.

Floors

Timber is a good choice for flooring as its lines, warmth and simplicity are conducive to both Japanese and Chinese style. For a starker, more pared-down effect, ceramic or terracotta tiles are also very effective, and their geometric shape adds interest and ordered pattern to a simple room. In areas where you want a bit more warmth or comfort underfoot, or simply want to break up the expanse of bare flooring, throw down a panel of natural flooring such as sisal or coir. In Japan, tatami mats, made out of compressed rice straw and edged with black tape, are used to soften the hard flooring.

Carpet is not out of the question in an oriental-themed room, but it should be a neutral colour and unpatterned. Ideal varieties are those with an inherent woven texture or pattern. Rugs and carpets with oriental-style decoration should be restricted to more flamboyant schemes, or to schemes in which they are the only element of pattern and colour. In fact, these rugs often work better in rooms where the designer simply wants to inject a small touch of the orient, rather than recreate a completely oriental look.

Right: ORIENTAL STYLE SUPPLIES A PERFECT THEME FOR A MODERN INTERIOR. COMBINE DECORATIVE CHINESE ARTEFACTS WITH THE COOL, UNCLUTTERED LINES OF TRADITIONAL JAPANESE INTERIORS FOR A SIMPLE, STYLISH BEDROOM.

1. Simple timber shutters diffuse the daylight and give privacy in the evening.

2. The black and white bedding is in perfect harmony with the room's oriental details. It is contemporary, yet its stylized form and motifs cement the oriental theme.

3. The richly stained timber flooring in this oriental-inspired bedroom is perfectly in keeping with its simple lines and calm, contemplative atmosphere.

4. A Chinese handpainted lacquered screen supplies colour and contrast to the room's ivory-painted walls.

5. A low-level oriental-style table can be seen in the room beyond, continuing this theme and sense of serenity into the remainder of the home.

Summing up the style

Index

Page numbers in *italic* refer to the illustrations

Picture Acknowledgements

Abode UK 19, 64 bottom, 64 top, 81, 108/109 centre, 153 right, 195, 198, 204/205 centre

Arcaid / Richard Bryant 162, 208/209, 211 bottom (Courtesy of the Georgian House, Edinburgh), / Mark Burgin/Belle 218/219, / Mark Fiennes 180, / Simon Kelly/Belle 34, 105, 135 right, / Ken Kirkwood 210, / Lucinda Lambton 190, 200/201 (Designer: David Harrison), 206/207, / Geoff Lung/Belle 46, / Julie Phipps 10, 66, 107, 129, / George Seper/Belle 55, / Rodney Weidland/Belle 113, / Alan Weintraub 18, 101

Laura Ashley 57& 95 right, 58, 69 & 77

Axiom Photographic Agency / Luke White 217 top

Coloroll Wallcoverings 13, 47

Crown Paints 33, 49, 85, 100, 102/103 & 115, 133

Crowson Fabrics 12, 37 right, 45 left, 134/135 centre

Ducal 151 right

Dulux Paints 2, 38, 74/75 & 86

EWA 6 & 160/161, 17, 26, 27, 30, 50, 51, 79 right, 82, 84, 91, 96, 97, 111 right, 118, 119, 120 centre, 122, 126, 127, 128, 130/131 & 139, 132, 137, 138, 142, 143, 146, 147, 148, 157, 164, 166/167, 168, 170/171, 172, 174, 176, 177, 178/179, 182/183, 184/185, 186, 188/189, 192, 196/197, 204 left, 212/213, 217 bottom

Harlequin Fabrics & Wallcoverings 68

Robert Harding Picture Library / Brian Harrison 110/111 centre, / IPC Magazines 150/151 centre, 152/153 centre , 214/215, / Tom Leighton 149, / James Merrell 144/145 & 154/155 centre, / Lizzie Orme 155 top right, 199 top, / David Parmiter 202/203

Nobilis-Fontan 40

Ikea 99 right

The Interior Archive / Tim Beddow 14/15, 31, 37 left, 59, 80, 125 top, 141, / Simon Brown 123, / Tim Clinch 45 right, 71, 76, / J Pilkington 136, 181 bottom, / Simon Upton 6, 88 & 98/99 centre, 104, 112/113 centre, / Andrew Wood 25, 62, 87 right, 114, 156, 165

Monkwells 42, 70, 109 right

Mike Newton 8/9, 32, 72/73, 158/159, 163, 169, 175, 181, 187, 193, 199, 205, 211, 216

Nordic Style Ltd 44, 187 left

Original Style Wall Tiles 194

Ornamenta 54

Osborne & Little 43 top, 60, 61

Debbie Patterson 16, 20, 28

Romo Fabrics & Wallcoverings Ltd 21

Arthur Sanderson & Co Ltd 48, 52, 53, 56, 67 & 93 right, 78/79 centre, 92/93 centre, 106

The Stock Market 36 / Tom Ives 24

Twyford 140

Mark Wilkinson 116/117 & 125 bottom, 121 right, 169

John Wilman Fabrics & Wallpapers 35, 43 bottom, 90, 94/95 centre